IN PRAISE OF *THE CHAPESS ZINE*

"Totally well-written, intelligent & unpretentious … an excellent read."

- Chris Kraus

"The Chapess began as a trickling stream, then a tidal wave. And now I can't imagine a time when you didn't exist."

- Alicia Rodriguez

"The Chapess is a sacred institution of friendship and punk and will always mean the world to me."

- Heather Dunlop

"The Chapess has influenced and inspired so much of myself, of my work. The range of content, of views, the sheer honesty makes it an important tribute to women everywhere. So much of what we consume as women does not reflect our identities at all. Mostly we're bombarded with ideas on how to be Better versions of ourselves. The Chapess provides vital reflections of women and women's work."

- Sara Sutterlin

"The Chapess is like a solace, a safe place...The fact that that place exists, if you really think about it, is a physical interruption and a real alternative to what those dominant narratives tell us; That our voices don't matter and to express them makes no difference to their power in shaping the world. Fuck that shit."

- Karis Upton

"I would actually suffocate and die in the suburbs if it wasn't for punk communities and outlets, online and off. The Chapess gives me air to breathe easy when I'm the only girl in town with the guts to wear black combat boots."

- Allison Maloney

"The Chapess is a loving/rage filled nest carved out by women for women to uphold women and give life/light to women. A crucial space/void for healing and not feeling so goddamn alone...It's a fucked up time in the world but damn, it's also a really exciting time to be alive and making art."

- Carolina Hicks

"A literary gun to the head of patriarchy and a triumphant nod to female-identifying nonconformists everywhere."

- Lydia Sviatoslavsky

What I most like about the Chapess is its poetics of inclusion. The Chapess is not a clique - you don't have to perform in any special way to be accepted. People are simply invited to share their creative expressions from the heart. Cherry Styles is a modern-day Gertrude Stein. She culls voices from the literary salon that is Tumblr. Those voices speak of community. It's a global consciousness-raising group made manifest through the printed pages of the Chapess. Cherry's vision and generosity of spirit make real the love, connection, and hope that exist in this world."

- Tracy Struck

GUT FLORA :
A CHAPESS ZINE
COLLECTION

edited by Cherry Styles

SYNCHRONISE
WITCHES PRESS

Published in 2016 by
Synchronise Witches Press
Manchester, UK
Printed by Ex Why Zed

thechapess.com
cherrystyles.co.uk

First printing July 2016

ISBN 978-0-9955100-0-5

SYNCHRONISE
WITCHES PRESS

JANE CHARDIET >

This is a sorry culture, babe. You have to make your own. - Alice Notley

The Chapess zine was started in 2011 by Zara Gardner as an accesible way to showcase the work of some of the amazing women artists and writers we knew and loved. Since then it has evolved from a crudely photocopied fanzine to a quarterly literary publication with an international readership.

In the early days many of the contributors were students we were working with (Zara and I met while working together in the art department of a sixth form college in Norfolk) or women within our immediate social circles. We wanted to give a voice to women like us, queer women, working class women, especially those in rural areas with limited resources, as we had been growing up - anyone feeling like they were out there doing their own thing, without a community. Both online and in print, the Chapess began to act as a point of contact and an open door to a worldwide network of creative women. With our feet firmly in our DIY roots we started helping other women to self publish through talks and workshops and hoped to lead by example as best we could. Many of our contributors are women sharing their work for the first time or in the very early stages of their writing careers, some of them experienced practicioners. There is no hierarchy of experience.

This book is a selected collection from the first nine issues of the zine. I could probably write a whole book about all the ways this project has changed my life for the better, but somehow this doesn't exactly seem like the place. The Chapess has always been collective venture, a project that has evolved with each new contributor, it belongs to all of us. Take what you need from this collection, share it with your friends.

Stay in touch,

Cherry x

BRIGID DEACON

7

I BELIEVE IN THE IMPORTANCE OF WOMEN CREATING SPACE FOR OTHER WOMEN. A CONTINUOUS SHARING OF ALL THINGS, A TRANSFERANCE OF POWER.

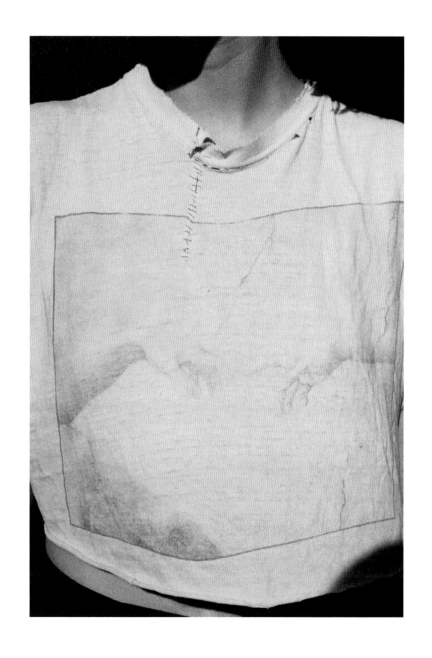

Style Like Eileen Myles

My girlfriend got me an Eileen Myles t-shirt at this Sister Spit event in Oakland, it's black with big purple letters reading "YOU'VE GOT THE STYLE EILEEN MYLES." I wore it for the first time in Palm Springs to a Dinah Shore White Party which is a party where everyone wears white. And Dinah Shore is this gross annual lesbian "weekend" for girls who want to fingerfuck in swimming pools, oil wrestle in wet t-shirts, drink their faces off and scream at each other in public. All the lesbian websites send reps to Dinah Shore so we were there like a bunch of pasty nerds at a football game, and I was there in my black pants and black Eileen Myles t-shirt at The White Party and then suddenly everything turned black and then I wasn't anywhere anymore. I was carried and I could hear things, like my friends saying I'd only had one drink and that my face was blue. Some minutes later in the hotel room as the EMTs were attaching things to me and announcing my alarming blood pressure I apparently garbled "it's over," to my friend Sarah. "It's all over, Sarah. This is it." Ha! She told me I'd said it a few times: "This is it, it's all over. It's all over. This is the end."

I think she thought I meant "my life." But although death felt remarkably possible at that moment, I didn't think "my life is over." I meant *the way I'd been living*. My 'poem' was over and hell had bottomed out. "I thought being an artist meant you had to do anything for the experience," Eileen Myles writes in *Inferno*. That's exactly what I'd done.

"In your twenties you just kind of chug along," Eileen Myles says, "dredging up feelings as you go." You "consider your behaviour just art, grist for the mill." So when I said "it's over," I was talking about the grist. Goodbye, mill.

I was being punished, I thought in my oxygen mask. For ignoring the voices in my head that'd told me I was doing it wrong and I'd be punished somehow if I kept that illegal job or started that business or moved there or spent that money or slept with him or did those five drugs at once or let her treat me like that. *But I'm in control of this chaos,* I'd insist. Even the hard parts. I'd lived through it, hadn't I?

But then I was lying on a hospital bed like an idiot with YOU'VE GOT THE STYLE EILEEN MYLES on my chest. It was embarrassing. "Earlier (24) I had decided it would be okay to kill myself. At 27 it was okay to live," Eileen Myles writes. Yes, me too, but I think I was 28, not 27. Not like I chose drama or instability, it just never scared me. Worst case scenario it'd be grist for the mill.

But if I, indeed, have the style like Eileen Myles, then those "bad" decisions weren't the self-indulgent decisions of a delusional dreamer or an elaborate display of self-sabotage. Those decisions weren't the decisions of an idiot, they were the decisions of a *writer.* This has been my work. All of it! This entire life! In a way I've always known this to be true, but I'd never heard a woman say so with such unapologetic swagger until I discovered Eileen Myles.

In Myles' 2000 book *Cool For You*, the narrator asks, "Why can't I be famous right now. Why can't I just act that way. Why can't I record everything down like my life counts." In *Inferno*, that's what Eileen Myles does.

"The artist must be entirely willing to live in the worst neighborhoods. Voluntarily the artist becomes poor and in that poverty she will begin to live in another time. A time outside of middle class America. The artist goes down to that other place for a while. Down like a roller coaster. Long enough to build a career. Then click click click pushing back up. The dirt of authenticity now on them and all the good training on the inside. But how, Lucy wonders, can the young working class man or woman ever accomplish this. Cause we're asking someone who grew up almost poor, to actually become poor. You're asking me to live in Somerville."

When Inferno starts, Eileen Myles is 18, I think, near Boston, in English class, with a teacher who has a beautiful ass and assigns her students to "write their own Inferno," after Dante. The teacher likes Eileen's submission so much that she reads it out loud to the class. Eileen smiles all the way home, having found her skill: "I could know myself, that's all. Some lazy thing I could always do because I was dumb and not normal, but special… something crazy — maybe that could be my job?"

She has this idea that knowing herself could be a job, that being a poet is a job. Nobody wants to pay you for that at first. So you hustle to make money to buy yourself time to write. But how I feel reading Eileen Myles is that the hustle doesn't just enable the writing, the hustle is part of the writing. The humility. That experience. My friends were too proud to accept expensive gifts from our wealthy friend. I wasn't. I was a writer, everything is a grant. Besides, I loved her.

The poet's job involves writing, but also serving drinks and washing floors. For Eileen; picking apples, selling slugs, filling out grant applications, befriending rich people. In New York I'd do any job besides a full-time office job. Think of your last-resort job. I did that job. Offices just seemed pointless. At least waiting tables something interesting might happen. I mean what the fuck was I even doing at Dinah Shore Weekend. It was so grotesque, I guess. So we could afford to come home and write about poetry.

But this is a big problem for women, obviously, making poetry a job. There's the money thing 'cause everyone has an opinion about your budget and thinks you're audacious for wanting to get paid to write. Generally speaking, also, most people think you're sort of silly, especially if you're a girl writing about yourself. Who wants to listen to a woman talk about herself! Why doesn't she just get a job at a bank.

Eileen Myles, like some other women I know who grew up not understanding why everyone treated them like girls, has that thing men have where they pop out of the womb already feeling important and necessary. All these little boys with mouths wide open telling stories we've heard a hundred times before. I'm not one of those women. I knew I was a girl and so I knew why I was being treated like one. "I was thinking today that I have spent my whole life trying to be a man," says Eileen Myles. "I'm sure you don't understand what I mean by that." Eileen Myles has that butch thing where she can play boys' games and have boy attitude but her heart is so female. It's killer. I mean she'll just slay you. I wanna be more like Eileen Myles. I mean she devotes an entire chapter to cunnilingus, eventually.

This whole book is yearning, yearning, yearning, sincerity in city-dirty fists, an odyssey that starts in Boston and derails to a large estate in Pennsylvania and hangs out in all the places you wish you'd been with all the people you wish you'd known in New York City— Patti Smith, an apartment in Soho "full of sluts" and Debbie Harry, St. Mark's Poetry Project, Kathy Acker, Nan Goldin. She went to New York to be a writer. So did I, but I thought admitting it would sound egotistical, wanting to be extraordinary.

There's a lot I love about *Inferno*: as a person, a lesbo, a woman, a former New Yorker, etc. But the main thing I took away from Inferno, which I read for the first time a year ago, was that it's okay to feel this way, content to be living and writing in that spot between sex and sadness. Being a writer. Being full of it. Being female. Having style like Eileen Myles.

How do I take myself seriously enough to say, "I am a writer, everything is a grant" without hearing everyone laugh at me, the entitled/lazy/stupid brat. How do I read my poem to the room without feeling like I should apologize afterward. As a woman, as a queer, as a writer, how do I stop worrying about what other people think and publish words like these: "no one asked me to have a life like this, to be a poet. It was my idea." Having her style is being hardened and sincere all at once, bathing in motor oil and rinsing off in a glass shower. It is riding Don Quixote's donkey. Yee-haw.

Several hours later I am still lying there in my Eileen Myles t-shirt in the Palm Springs Emergency Room. I've been resuscitated. I owe them something like $7,000, which seems obnoxious. Their tests were inconclusive. Maybe it was dehydration? They gave me a pamphlet about fainting spells. Did I want a brain scan? I couldn't afford it. Was I employed? I was not. They'd send me some papers so I could ask the government to foot the bill. Sure.

I'm tangled up in all my imagined probable causes, each one eternally possible and impossible. What was I being punished for? I'd never know.

So we went back to the quiet hotel room and I got into bed in my Eileen Myles t-shirt and my underpants. Everyone was sleeping and I felt like a deer.

"It would be embarrassing behavior if the person was real," writes Eileen Myles. "But he wasn't. He was a writer."

RIESE BERNARD

ALBA YRUELA

On Kate Zambreno's Heroines, Being Too Much and Taking Up Space

A few months ago, as I was furiously reading and re-reading Kate Zambreno's *Heroines* (Semiotext(e)), my new homeopathic remedies arrived in the mail. One of the dropper bottles had been marked by my practitioner: "1 drop every night, or as needed for fear of being too much." The timing was almost too good. In *Heroines*, Zambreno writes about the women of modernism. She reclaims and reinterprets the biographies of people like Jane Bowles and Zelda Fitzgerald and Vivien(ne) Eliot, who were pathologized, diagnosed as hysterics for their excesses of emotion, even as all that Being Too Much was appropriated by their husbands as material, for use in their works—books that would later be canonized as Great American Literature.

Reading Zambreno's meditations on this kind of pathologizing, I thought a lot about the state of Being Too Much versus the desire—and what also, often, feels like the feminist responsibility—to Take Up Space. We talk a lot about Taking Up Space. Why don't the women in the audience at the event ask any questions? Why do I introduce myself as a waitress instead of saying I'm a writer? But there's a strange disconnect somewhere between Being Too Much and yet not Taking Up Enough Space, which sound like they should at least resemble each other, or that one should be en route to the other. I think that I am Too Much, and it feels like I am oozing all over the floor. I tell myself that I need to learn to Take Up Space, and Taking Up Space seems like it should look like something more solid, something that knows how to express its well-formed opinions calmly and yet with force.

Heroines is passionate and sprawling and unapologetic; it infuriated and obsessed me. I read and I underlined and I copied out whole paragraphs and I felt so angry and then I had this awful moment where I realized that I might be the man in my own life telling me that I'm Too Much. I was nodding along as Zambreno called out the patriarchal mores that tell women they're crazy, but the truth is that I have swallowed so much of that myself that I am the first person to call myself crazy; I will beat you to the punch.

18

Heroines provoked a lot of reaction—much of it positive, some of it less so. Jessica Winter, writing in the fall issue of Bookforum, exhorts Zambreno to pick up a newspaper. In the wake of the recession, she says, aren't most people just worried about paying the rent? Zambreno's writing, says Winter, "reads like a misogynist's broad parody of a feminist artist: slapping at shadows, barking comebacks at scarecrows." But not everything can be quantified with statistics like the VIDA counts; you can't graph what kinds of emotional outbursts are allowed. Does this mean we can't talk about it?

That's the thing about the silencing of women writers: part of its violence lies in the fact that it will never make the news. In the fact that you can read feminist texts and make arguments and feel alive in the face of another woman's bravery, but somewhere deep inside there is still an obedient voice that says *Yes but you're crazy, you're Too Much*, and it can be loud enough to effectively shut you up. I know where that voice comes from; I know why I shouldn't listen to it. And so I feel that I am supposed to be past this. I am embarrassed to admit that I am not entirely there yet.

Of course, it's important to talk facts about the realities of institutionalized misogyny and where women are getting published and how often (and how) they are getting reviewed; these are important conversations. But a riskier and equally important conversation is the one about all those buried lessons that we are afraid to admit still affect us.

Because sometimes it's just scary, to feel so much, and then it's scary to own up to that fear. Sometimes I'm scared of myself, the force of the feelings I often can't contain, and I wish I weren't scared and I struggle with myself over it, and I don't know how to get out from underneath that fear sometimes. I don't even know how to confront this fear, even as I rationally know where it comes from and what it means and why I should overcome it. I read back my own notebooks suspiciously, wondering if I was really being honest. I get carried away in an argument and lash out, expressing how I really feel, and then I regret it for days, squirming and anxious as I relive my own honesty. I am still battling that bred-in need to please and be loved.

And so, my reaction, when I read in *Heroines* about Lucia Joyce throwing a chair across the room, shrieking, "I AM THE ARTIST!", is to think about how fucking great that is. How she was not telling herself that she was crazy—she was saying *Fuck you for not listening to me*. I feel a rush of release reading about Zelda burning her clothes in the bathtub, Vivien(ne) throwing her nightgown out the window. The men in their lives censored their work, institutionalized them, but these women weren't biting their tongues, containing themselves. At least in those moments, they didn't wash their faces and fold their hands and smile like pretty ladies; they set the place on fire.

(Of course, for Zelda and Lucia and Vivien(ne) and so many of the other women about whom Zambreno writes, the consequences for lashing out were very real, and in many cases tragic. As Zambreno points out, the men were allowed to own their eccentricities, their excesses; it went along with their genius. But the women weren't forgiven; there was no room for their excess. Can I applaud those moments in which these women did cry out, push back, spill over, despite the policing of their behavior, without glamorizing the breakdown?)

Zambreno quotes R.D. Laing: "To invalidate can stir one to violence." It becomes a terrible cycle. One is violent because one has been invalidated; one is invalidated because one has been violent:

Compose yourself. Compose yourself. They are supposed to hold it in. To control themselves. Perhaps the fury is one's own containment. If one wasn't so contained, one wouldn't be so furious.

"I found the emotionless condition a great strain, all the time. I used to think I should burst out and scream and dance," writes Vivien(ne).

If there was room to get emotional and not fear being written off because of it; if I didn't struggle to control those emotions in order to be taken seriously, and then become angry at the thought of silencing myself, and then silence that anger and so on in a continual loop; basically, if I could Take Up Space in a way in which I could still be myself, then I have a feeling that it all wouldn't seem like Being Too Much anymore. I wouldn't feel like I was spilling over the boundary of "appropriate behavior," if that boundary were a little more malleable, a little less judgmental. There wouldn't be the same urge to smash up against it or kick it down. And since I don't see permission to alter those boundaries coming from anywhere else, maybe I just have to give it to myself.

I love this story Kate Durbin tells, in a conversation with Zambreno at Her Kind, about Lady Gaga and Marina Abramović:

There was this interview Gaga did with SHOWSTUDIO, wherein Marina Abramović called in—many celebs called in. Abramović asked Gaga the question: "Who creates limits?" Gaga answered, "We do," and then she said to the interviewer: "You see how simple her [Abramović's] question was? That's because she's fucking free." The interviewer asked Gaga to explain, and she said, after gushing about seeing "The Artist is Present" in NYC, and gushing about "Rhythm O," Abramović's famous performance wherein she let the audience abuse her, almost to the point of death, without surrendering or bowing her head: "That bitch trusts herself, and she trusts her art."

To me, to be a woman, an artist, and to be free, the bitch has to trust herself, has to trust her art.

Chris Kraus recently said in an interview that the work she loves the most is "the work that doesn't try to make itself loveable." I, too, love this kind of work. I find it brave and exciting and truthful and important. And I admire it because it's hard to break those habits. To realize that the love and approval of someone else is not going to get you to a place of trusting yourself. And any worthwhile work is not going to come out of any other place. This is, for me, tied to the idea of giving permission to yourself, of deciding to Take Up Space in a way that doesn't stifle. Trusting yourself to make your own limits.

The final section of *Heroines* discusses the space afforded by the internet, the world of feminist blogs and Tumblrs, for criticism that is free to be subjective, to have feelings. In these spaces, one can find an ongoing conversation that delves into much of what I've been discussing here, and, in fact, goes further, is more confrontational, takes more risks. I am saying nothing new in wondering about how to do away with a dichotomy in which one isn't Taking Up Enough Space and yet is Too Much. The fear that persists, the struggle with that learned longing to please and be loved—these are rather unoriginal confessions, but what if that's the important thing about them? That I am not the first to say this, but am going to talk about it anyway. I feel uncertain and vulnerable, writing this. There is no data with which to arm myself, it's all so subjective, but does that mean I can't talk about it? I want to figure out what Taking Up Space could look like for me, and I don't really know how else to do that except for out-loud. Even if it's boring, even if it's unoriginal, even if I'm less articulate than I want to be, less certain. Maybe I'm already Taking Up Space, just by Talking About It Anyway.

I had this idea, a few months back, that red lipstick would help somehow. That maybe I had been a tomboy as a child because girly things like makeup were a kind of Taking Up Space that I didn't have the guts for. And so I went to Sephora for the first time in my life and one of the women working there noticed me shuffling around the lipsticks, awkward and lost, and took me by the hand. "Is this your first red?" she asked, solemnly.

Heroines gives itself permission to be the kind of work of criticism that sometimes has tears in its eyes, that is a little red in the face by the end of the argument because it just loves the books so much; it is so invested. It is these qualities that make the book feel vast, voluptuous, while at the same time focused. It is heavily researched, sharply observed. It Takes Up Space but it does so on its own terms. And that Zambreno sets this example and does so boldly is, for me, one of the most exciting things about the work. "Perhaps," she writes, "it's okay that I am porous, sensitive, excessive, emotional. But we do need to be brave. We do need to write *despite* it all." Make our own limits. Talk about it anyway.

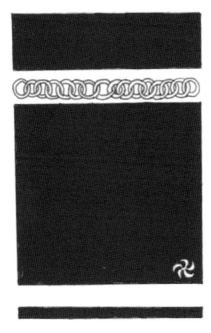

MAPPING THE INTERNAL LANDSCAPES:

ZINE-MAKING AS COPING
SELF-PUBLISHING AS PROOF THAT YOU WERE
SELF-EXPRESSION AS ↗ THERE AND NOW
                     YOU'RE HERE

THE DOCUMENTATION OF RELEASE OF EXPRESSION OF: YOUR THOUGHTS, FEELINGS, HIGHS, LOWS, NUMBS, BACKTRACKS, FUCK-UPS, VICTORIES, DAYDREAMS, NIGHT-MARES, GOALS, IDEAS, QUESTIONS, POISONS, MYSTERIES, DESIRES, DISGUSTS, HEALING WORDS

is AS essential as expelling waste from your system, LIKE DIGESTION, like self-cleaning ORGANS, LIKE PISSING, LIKE CRYING

YOUR MIND NEEDS TO DIGEST OR ELSE YOU WILL GET POISONED AND YOU BECOME CLOGGED & STUCK

DO NOT WAIT FOR SOMEONE TO VALIDATE YOU OR YOUR CREATIVE VALUE/WORTH! DO THAT YOURSELF, RIGHT HERE, READ THESE WORDS LIKE A SPELL:

I RELEASE MYSELF FROM MY OWN RESTRICTING THOUGHTS. IF I CAN THINK, IF I CAN FEEL, I CAN EXPRESS. MY MIND'S OUTPUT IS VALID AND VALUABLE BECAUSE I AM THE ONLY ME THAT WILL EVER BE.

24

I OFTEN FEEL LIKE I EXIST WITHIN
THE VACUUM OF MYSELF -
MY ANXIETY SEES AND REACTS TO THE CHAOS
ALL AROUND ME BUT MY DEPRESSION AND
EXISTENTIAL DREAD CONVINCE ME THAT
I'M ALONE IN THAT CHAOS.

I WEAR MY TRAUMA AND
ACCUMULATED PAIN AS A
THICK DIRT SUIT - THE DIRT
PLUGS UP MY EARS SO I CAN
ONLY HEAR MY OWN HEART
BEATING - THE DIRTS GETS INTO
MY EYES AND MY VISION TURNS
TO MUD - I'LL MAKE THE MISTAKE OF
CATCHING A GLIMPSE OF MY OWN REFLECT-
ION ON A SURFACE OR MIRROR AND SCREECH:

BLANK NUMB EXPRESSION

I'M
CAUGHT
IN THE
PARALYZING
HEADLIGHTS OF
EXISTING!

Oh my
God
is that
me?

FU CK.
YU CK.

AM
I
REA-
LLY
A
PER-
SON?

SBTL
CLNG

SO HEY, IF YOU'RE READING THIS AND CAN
RELATE: YOU'RE NOT ALONE IN FEELING ALONE!
BEING A PERSON IS A VERY DENSE PROJECT
AND WHEN YOU'RE AWARE, IT CAN BE REALLY
GNARLY. BUT I LOVE YOU! LET'S STAY ALIVE.

It's summer and these are the things you leave me with: the smell of come and burning wood on my bed sheets, stiff muscles around my waist and my body is trembling for days. After you leave and I'm alone, I whisper to myself the things I dream you would ask me, and what I would ask you. I'm muttering conversations between myself and I, imagining a "you" on the other end. But you and I don't talk. I'm foolish enough to think that there is something here. I add up our once-a-month encounters, (you call me at your convenience, *I am the one who waits*), our unintentional rendezvous arising out of summer lust, drinking clear tequila in the grimy Atlanta heat; sharing joints outside of house shows and speaking in each other's ears in the back of venues in the dark; and having been fond of each other for a couple of years prior - we always passed each other and *I always felt some kind of recognition from you.*

Are you going to be a dirty punk forever?
What do you yearn for?

A game of sustainability: How can I give you something I don't have? I want more than this but I know this is the perfect, tragic space. We're floating in an untainted space of intimate expression, residing outside of public judgment. No expectations, no accountability. I can't ask you of anything, and because I have no witness.

Sometime in the Spring: I'm in an airplane flying over the West coast. *Faded west coast skies, faded east coast girl.* I drank two glasses of red wine before boarding the plane hoping to pass out instead of yearning for your hands on my thighs for six hours, as I'm suspended in the air surrounded by strangers. I'm squirming in my seat, thinking of how your sad brown eyes make me come and how dark that is. Instead of living out my fear of moaning aloud, everything fades to black and I'm pulled into sleep.

The woman sitting next to me on the plane is eager to make conversation. My head is pounding but I oblige because of her kind eyes. *You can move across the country. You are young.* She tells me that she has been taking care of her ailing mother for eight months in the Valley. She asks me what I will be studying, and I tell her Cultural Studies. That is important to study, especially now. I don't know what she means by that, and I don't remember how our conversation ends.

A girl gets sick of a Rose. – Gwendolyn Brooks. Why do people make the mistake of thinking I'm good? I'm bad like you. You ask me, *what is a woman like you doing with a drunk like me?* You ask me, *where is your boyfriend?* It's hard for you to believe I'm bad like you, seething anger and booze, staying out late for the possibility of things. Like you, I'm keeping you around until you're useful for me. *You can call me bad names if that's your thing*, I tell you, among other things. The shameful unspoken things that get me off surface, and then disappear again, and you don't even notice.

I've made some rules for myself to parcel it all out. I only go to their places – I don't want the memory of them in my bed, or in my room, and I don't want them to know my bedroom culture. I don't ask them about their day or their feelings unless they first ask me about mine (a rare occurrence). I don't ask them of anything, really. Using a condom is the only card you have. I leave shortly after they fall asleep, and always before the sun comes up. Leave before they ask you to leave. When the timing is right, I am lucky enough to catch the moon in the daylight.

Why drive?

The metro is faster anyways
he says until   sweating stuck
          on the   south-bound 4   everyone's
                    melting into   each-other's lap.

I drink,   we drink to   be funnier
          to reappear

& I start telling him about the   Villa of Mysteries
          Pompeii
          oranges   red and purple walls   corpse flowers everywhere
          orgies   & sacrifices,

          rituals of initiation now a
                              ruin   under ash.   I see

                    eros
                              holding a mirror to a young woman
          while a horse   plays the lyre

          or so I imagine.

     I say

          I'd like to think there is a place where
                    everything could
                              exist   simultaneously.

          He

                              is not colored by these visions,

                    & unlacing his shoes

                              only says

          this   will   be   bad   for   you.

JULIA WOHLSTETTER

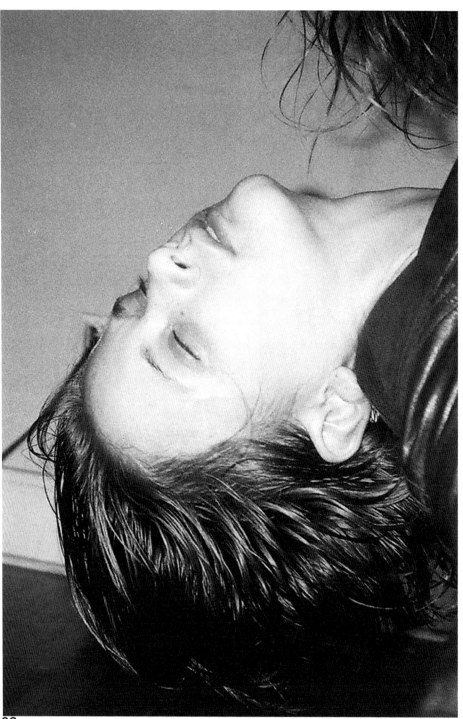

WARNING: EXPLICIT CONTENT

CHARLOTTE McHARG

Ex-boyfriends and ugly feelings, family skeletons and panic attacks, choking self-doubt mingled with soaring grandiosity: this is the bread and wine of confessional blogging. At xoJane, Cat Marnell describes her pettiness toward her co-workers at the website and details her struggle to kick her addiction to Adderall in real time. In a personal blog that eventually became an e-book, Dodie Bellamy draws on art and theory to explore the emotional aftermath of a romantic affair with a Buddhist teacher. And on Tumblr, writer and PhD student Kara Jesella archives the detritus of her relationship and breakup, including a miscarriage and a stay in a psychiatric ward—and analyzes the feminist underpinnings of the entire endeavour.

For me, this is a gift. All I have ever wanted is for interesting people to tell me their stories – the messy, honest ones that normally come along only after a few drinks. That's why I love memoirs and Sylvia Plath and Audre Lorde and PostSecret and Joni Mitchell. The confessional voice, done with attention to craft, is one of the best antidotes I know to isolation. Not coincidentally, as far as I can tell the majority of the bloggers currently practicing it are women. Also not coincidentally, the confessional voice—both historically and in the present—has haters without end.

I believe that women writers are drawn to the confessional voice because they are not supposed to speak their pain. The same goes for people who are nonwhite or GLBTQ or disabled or otherwise on societal margins.

Confession is only necessary where there is repression, where it serves the interests of those in power to persuade those who aren't to maintain their silence. And so confessional blogging, like confessional poetry and confessional novels before it, is a political act. Lorde expounds on the necessity of personal disclosure, writing, "Your silences will not protect you [. . .] What are the tyrannies you swallow day by day and attempt to make your own, until you will sicken and die of them, still in silence? We have been socialized to respect fear more than our own need for language." Lorde's criticism applies to the personal just as much as the political, because the two are inseparable in her life and in everyone's.

Enter the ex-boyfriends.

Bellamy's blog and book The Buddhist is rife with the embarrassment of personal disclosure. It is embarrassing for her to admit how often she thinks of her former lover, a Buddhist teacher. She tries to stop writing about him over and over again: "So, I'm saying goodbye to the Buddhist vein here," she says, with half her book still to go. "I already said that, but I mean it this time." (She doesn't.) It's embarrassing for her to continue mourning the relationship long past its expiration date, and even more embarrassing to blog about it. Whereas the mantle of what she calls Real Writing might lend her heartbreak cultural credibility and make writing about it more acceptable, blogging won't protect her from judgement. In fact, it exposes her further. Yet she grows committed to documenting the relationship and breakup when she considers who and what culturally-imposed silence on personal drama serves. Bellamy writes,

"This business of women not suffering in public, of having a gag order when it comes to personal drama, such as a break up, connects back to larger histories of suppression [. . .] a harkening back to the whole notion that domestic space is private, what happens behind closed doors stays behind closed doors, and somewhere buried in there is the history of the wife being owned by her man and therefore she better keep her trap shut, and bourgeois notions of suffering with dignity—or dignity itself, how oppressive a value is that?"

Bellamy gives her Buddhist anonymity, including few identifying details, but she painstakingly refuses to give herself the false comforts of dignity. A dignified person, after all, appears assured of herself and her place in the world—low on self-doubt, slightly elevated above the ordinary scrambling of humanity. Gwyneth Paltrow-esque. But Bellamy wants to be honest about her desperation and confusion, the waves of longing and fury and acceptance that crash over her without end. So she replays past conversations with the

36

Buddhist, the contradictions between his beliefs and actions: how he gave money to a homeless person who asked for it as his spirituality says he should, but how afterward he complained about the likelihood that the man would use it for drugs. Their awkward lovemaking is on the table, as are his lies about his relationship status and his attempts to keep the relationship on un-solid ground and thereby maintain control. (A tiny detail to which Bellamy, rightly, assigns great meaning: after signing many emails in a row with love, he switches to "with warmest regards," without warning, just to keep her guessing.) She's an emotional detective trying to solve the mystery of what exactly happened between them, who he was, who she became with and after him.

The Buddhist struck a chord with many readers. There are plenty of reasons why, but among them is the fact people feel messy inside with great frequency, which makes them feel alone. This is particularly true when they don't hear anyone else admitting how messed up they are. To find a writer talking eloquently and openly about their 3 AM fears and bête noires and interpersonal despair is to find a friend in the wilderness — not least because Bellamy, in refusing dignity, finds a new form of it, one that's large enough to encompass all of her.

Kara Jesella's Tumblr gives a name to the project both she and Bellamy undertake: radical vulnerability. Jesella explains the genesis of the term: "radical vulnerability, here, is about questioning the self-contained liberal subject, not about self-disclosure, though i think there is something about admitting that other bodies are a part of you that makes it related to self-disclosure after all." In other words, when Jesella brings other people into her Tumblr narrative—most notably her ex-boyfriend, but also her parents and brother and friends and professors and colleagues and feminist/queer theory heroes—she challenges the idea that it's even possible to tell your own story without telling the story of others too.

In Bird By Bird, Annie Lamott tells aspiring writers, "Remember that you own what happened to you." In this spirit, Jesella posts Gmail correspondences between herself and her ex, recounts past fights and scans old birthday cards. He comes off pretty badly, I have to say, but it's his own words and actions that incriminate him. (Confessional writing has to be committed to telling the truth to the best of its ability; otherwise it's just a libel lawsuit in sheep's clothing.) Reading her Tumblr is a reminder of how unfair it can be for a person to maintain an unblemished public front while acting callously and cruelly in private.

Of course, this kind of disclosure isn't for everyone, and there are any number of sensible reasons why a person might elect to keep quiet about personal drama, particularly the kind that involves relationships. But Jesella's defense is completely legitimate. "'[Y]ou're hurting me' and 'ethics' and 'discretion' are such obvious coverups—by self-identified feminist men—for behaviour both atrocious and foolish that they don't want exposed or theorized." In that vein, she offers the example of a fight she has with her ex about her blog:

last night he told me he has tried to be ethical in the wake of our relationship; the implication being that i have not. i told him that earlier this week i found an email from him sent exactly a week after my miscarriage, when i was home alone with gynecological pains, with the all-caps subject line "YOU ARE NOT THE ONLY ONE WHO GETS TO BE HURT." it proceeded to tell me that i was not proactively looking out for his post-miscarriage feelings (actually, i really was). he also refused to tell me when we could see each other that week and then accused me of not wanting to spend time with him when i replied that though i really wanted to be with him, if he couldn't tell me, i would make plans with other people, because i was feeling really fragile, not to mention i was scared about what was going on physically, and didn't want to be alone right then. what is unethical, to me, is his thinking it was okay to treat me this way ever, but especially after a fraught surgery. what is ethical is my talking about it. i didn't get to the psych ward all by myself and i'm not the only person who has been in a situation like this. [. . .] and i guess i was really in love with him once, which counts for something when making decisions, but i will always be in love with my feminist ethics more. and i meant what i said: i would feel fine if he talked about our relationship. i have nothing to hide.

No doubt, there are risks that come with radical vulnerability–particularly online, where anyone can read what you write and names and identities are eminently Google-able. Jesella risks alienating people in her life, although the fact that she's in a feminist academic community means that she's more likely than most to be around people who will understand the reasoning and intent behind her project. Heather Armstrong (aka Dooce) lost her job at a software company because she wrote about the higher-ups. Blogger Hysteriarama summarizes the risks and rewards of confessional blogging: "over-sharing is totes a legit political tactic and super necessary and repression is boooooooring (I know there's another side to this where over-sharing marginalizes you and you compromise to survive and work through systems that will get you closer to something that isn't totally alienating but right now I'm bleeding and hungry and broke and my house is annoying and I'm feeling really negate negate negate)."

With these risks in mind, Jesella and Bellamy show that confessional blogging, at its heart, is about transgressing social boundaries. That's certainly part of Marnell's rock star anti-heroine aesthetic as well. Among the writers in this article, though, Marnell is the outlier. Jesella and Bellamy, if they don't already read each other's work, would very likely feel an affinity with one another. My guess is that Marnell wouldn't be an easy fit for either of them. Her article on practicing unsafe sex was met (understandably) with protests throughout the feminist blogosphere. Another post on losing weight through a juice cleanse drew criticism from bloggers who noted that the subject gets really complicated when it's being written by a woman with a history of eating disorders, particularly without acknowledgment of that history.

The objections to Marnell are also her draw. Not only is she willing to talk about any number of taboo and highly personal subjects, she's quick to take an unpopular position—though not, I think, just for provocation's sake. As a beauty editor, it's Marnell's job to talk about products that women use to maintain or enhance appearances. The energy in her writing comes from the tension between the products she's writing about—black eyeliner and detanglers and coconut-scented body lotions—and the way she writes about

39

them, which constantly exposes and discloses massive contradictions.

Most beauty copy is chipper and sprightly, with no acknowledgment of the complex social histories brewing within a tube of pink champagne lip gloss. But Marnell's confessions unleash conflict. There's the contrast between the classically pretty surface of Marnell herself—blonde and slim and doe-eyed—and her chaotic, egomaniacal interior. There's the discontinuity of the punk-rock look of her designer-made boots and purses. She's both a high-achieving professional with a dream job, having dutifully worked her way up the editorial ladder at a number of top fashion magazines, and a nightmare employee who writes regularly about crying in HR meetings, blowing off work, missing deadlines, and jotting off notes on the plane to let her boss know she's taking a working vacation in Miami, effective immediately.

By burying the beauty product lede beneath thousands of words on her stays in mental health clinics and her estranged relationship with her father, Marnell opposes the beautification of her own life and personality. But at the same time, she acknowledges that she's still creating an image of herself as she wishes to be seen. She writes, "Also part of being an editor is editing your own Narrative, your own Truth, and I am always presenting a Cat that is far more loveable, generous and charming than who I really am lately." Though Cat makes this confession in an article that tries to expose her own worst impulses, it also points to her skillful technique. Confessional blogging sheds so many protective layers—the overcoat of the fiction label, the sweater of print, the hoodie of experimental form – that it's easy to believe writers are simply pouring themselves onto the page without premeditation or revision or considerations of style. But a good confessional blogger knows how to give an online community the sense that they're gaining private access to her most visceral feelings while still shaping the story.

There's a level of privilege that comes with confession. Marnell, Bellamy, and Jesella are all white, middle-class(ish) women in creative and intellectual communities where they can feel confident enough to expose themselves (selectively) without fearing that they'll lose everything. Writers with less privilege surely use the confessional voice as well, but as a platform to speak truth to power it's hobbled by the question of who ends up paying for it.

Still, the idea behind confessional writing, as expressed by pioneers like Lorde and Adrienne Rich, is to work toward a world that doesn't punish people for revealing the full spectrum of their humanity, for telling how and where they've been hurt. "There must be those among whom we can sit down and weep," Rich writes, "and still be counted as warriors." That's what I love about the stances taken by Marnell and Bellamy and Jesella. At first glance, it may look like they're lying on the ground in tears. And maybe they are. But take another look, and you'll see that they're heading toward something dark and roiling. They're not afraid of it, because they know what's inside. Now they're sprinting.

Professor Present

Today I imagine you looking for my tracks. Listening for clues as if I want you back.

You enjoy my tweets.
You think I write for you.
You reply in places I don't return to.

Today I see the world the way you taught me to. A way I can't separate from myself. (You really got me good)

You know you're not allowed to signal to me.
You know that *Cuttlefish* is the password.

Today I hope another student has taken my place. I couldn't have been the only one.

You can't imagine that I don't think of you.
You enjoy being right.
You can be patient.

Today I will only meet you again at your deathbed, the only time you can't come after me.
Unless you get me first, *Cuttlefish.*

Professor Past

Professor professor mister dad wannabe yes I'd like you to be.

I wonder if I will ever tell anyone that I took all of the words you wrote,
framed them under my signature, and signed my name on top.

I worked for that diploma. I stole so wisely and sucked deeply.
No one noticed.
Too busy grading life.

I've carved out plenty of guilt. I wanted someone else to have given it to me. Shamed me.

Pass over some of that blame. But that's impossible when nobody knows.
Nobody knows the cock I curled around my finger, the words I borrowed.

Professor professor tell me I'm smart. We know I'm pretty, we heard it in the corridors.
No rush I'll squeeze it out of you.

living with a long term illness is often lonely. so come along and be with others who understand

(mum had underlined passages in her copy of Jeanette Winterson's 'Written on the Body'. i borrowed the book when i was sixteen and didn't finish it. i was embarrassed. she underlined something like: *i work hard for this relationship because i fear for it*. i think i've probably attached, over the past eight years, a lot of arbitrary significance to this. i worry about mum. she's had ME for a long time. she does a lot of emotional work, which is passed down through daughters, i'm sure of it. *i work hard for this relationship because i fear for it*. i wonder when it was that she had underlined this sentence. i looked for the book last time i visited and it had disappeared)

believes her own bullshit

of course we retreat to the undigestible, the hard to swallow/ask the goddesses, ask the vampires, ask the planets because there is no room for our anger in that senior staff white male university educated lecturer's office

ALICIA RODRIGUEZ

{ghost emoji}

Hi. Remember when we were spooky as hell lovers and would text each other at exactly the same time to say I love you? Your thumb moving at the same speed as my thumb but one hundred and twenty eight point seven miles away. Tap tap tap on that Nokia 3310 like an insect's jaw twitching in delight.

I would've sent you an emoji of a ghost after that but emojis didn't exist then. It was 2005. Nothing existed in 2005. None of the people alive today were even born in 2005. There was just you and me.

You were a smooth dirty stomach the colour of pepper. I was the clammy ring of a wrist where a leather watchstrap had sweated out the smell of vinegar. You'd kiss the tip of my nose and I'd kiss your forehead and we'd taste like salt in each other's mouths. Bodies are just condiments and it's true that without your body I couldn't really taste or even feel anything at all.

I would wait two weeks for the forty-eight hours when you were a silhouette above me in the half-light. So long to wait for the moment when you would wipe the sloppy end of your dick on dirty pastel curtains that were as thin and brittle as old paper. And maybe they shattered when you did that and maybe everything shattered when you did that.

In your sweat soaked bed we hastily constructed a tiny fragile palace made from the smell of our bodies and a series of involuntary noises. And in that palace you became a ghost who haunted my insides. A ghost crawling all over my skeleton and using your ghost fingers and ghost mouth to press at the buttons on my spine. The buttons on my spine sent electricity directly to my brain and then spook fuelled brain electricity settled in puddles all over us.

For two out of fourteen days I could slot myself inside you but you were so disgusted and I was so embarrassed when you took a lil lump of damp toilet paper out of your mouth after going down on me. Your tongue ran over the

46

ridges of your gums, panicked that a piece of me would wedge in your sturdy molars forever.

You walked faster than me when we were out and wouldn't wait when the shoes I'd bought to impress you blistered my feet. I knew then that you would never revel in the smell of the juice squeezed from my blisters. In very small corners I milked the pus from my foot. I touched the crispy wave of flesh left behind when the blister burst and dried out and I whispered all of my secrets to that yellowy white sheet of skin as slight and lined as a map. I'd written you a love story with my body but you didn't want to read it.

I tried to make myself prettier but some how I always looked like a clown whose face has collapsed because of a serious but not life threatening medical condition. Everything in the world shrank to the size of your room and I shrank myself to the size of a bird or a bug or the stain on the rug from something that had dripped out from inside me. I wondered how you could sleep so soundly next to me when I was wide awake and watching the Nokia 3310 light up with messages every five minutes or so.

It would've carried on that way forever, taking a train across the Pennines every other weekend if you hadn't gotten an STI from a Danish exchange student who drank pints of milk for refreshment and fun.

Later I'd look at her MySpace and try to decide if she had better eyebrows than me. It seemed so important to win in that way. If only my face could produce hair of a certain thickness in a certain way then the bone and flesh of my chest would be able to grow back, my spine would strengthen and it would be easier to look at my skin.

Because I had so much love in my guts for you that I just about shit myself every time I saw you waiting on the platform. Sadness can be unbearable sometimes but that's about all I can say on the subject.

After becoming dehydrated on a train all that was left of you and me was the thick discharge like a smear of porridge sitting in my gusset, the itching and the tests and the look of disapproval from the middle-aged nurse who knew my mother socially. You gave me the gift of an overwhelming feeling that I would never ever really know another person. And we became just like everybody else really. Later, my body found so many other bodies that fitted together with it so nicely and I am sure that your body did too.

It was only the eventual invention of the ghost emoji that would remind me how I once fitted so well into yours. The ghost sticks out its tongue and holds up its arms to surrender and terrify. A big eye like yours. A small eye like mine. It's spooky as all heck and it's just like us. Bye.

MARIE
BONAPARTE
A LIFE

CELIA BERTIN

SAHAR GILANI

The mental breakdown was necessary, or at least I'm too much of a romantic to indulge in downward spirals. I had spent the past 30 days in the middle of nowhere in Mexico videotaping myself doing karaoke and watching a conversation between Sharon Hayes and Lawrence Weiner over and over. I wasn't speaking to anyone and a transference of affection became placed on a dead bird that had suddenly appeared and disappeared in my backyard the first day I arrived. I thought the omen was a certain death symbol, but it evolved into a mascot of my relishing in seclusion. The bird was never named and took the place of a half memory of a failed relationship back in New York. It was now the last week that I had in Mexico, and in a pathetic attempt to re-assimilate into having to speak to people, I went to Mexico City.

I had booked a hostel in what I imagined to be the midtown of DF, but instead of advertisements there were cathedrals. They evoked the same gestures out of tourists, but instead of a backdrop of the Mecca of sugar snacks, tourists posed for photos in a similar fashion with tear stained eyes masked in incense.

I walk around, I'm wearing a giant jumpsuit that I call my baby suit. It's not sexy at all, but I look good and I wear it whenever I travel. In New York, my baby suit yields many compliments except when I am on a bike. The thin draped fabric inflates as I pedal, the color is that of a cheap fat suit. While in motion it gives the illusion of an obese woman on a miniature bicycle.

So I'm feeling good about being with other people. There are many couples kissing in the streets, children running while smiling, nobody has their hands in their pockets. It's a beautiful day with beautiful stores. My favorite store is filled with rotating wedding dresses, silk flowers reflecting the neon lights of the displays. The city is busy, a welcome change from the sleepy town I would buy little cakes and cheap wine in. I'm alone and it's terribly safe. I feel resentment for all my relatives who advised me not to wear earrings. All the women are wearing earrings. I'm wearing a baby suit.

I'm thirsty. I stop into a corner store to get some water. I'm smiling as I pick up my water and I notice a gentleman staring at me with disgust and confusion. He slithers through the tiny aisles as I decide on what kind of nuts I want to chew on. I make my way up to the counter and he approaches me. "Do you think you're funny?" he asks me in Spanish. I notice his purple velvet pants and paisley vest. I wonder if he is an actor. You can never trust actors. "Excuse me?" I say. "Why aren't you dressed like a woman? You are doing your body no favors! Are you a joke?" he says. "Fuck you! Who are you to tell me about my body!" I yell back at him. I exit the store moving my hips however I please. I wonder where the feminists hang out here.

For my stay in Mexico I've been reading Sex and Repression in a Savage Society, a study examining the sexual habits of Melanesian and British families. In Melanesia, the family structure is matrilineal which Bronislaw Malinowski argues leads to primordial Edipus tendencies that are repressed, but maintained. This plasticity of instincts can be manifested in many ways, one being masking the complex with deflecting and ignorance. I've made up my mind that this actor was in love with his mother, and my dressing like a baby became a trigger for his suppressed, misunderstood feelings.

While back at my hostel I become friends with Humberto, a visitor from Colombia who owns a small camping space where he tells me it is the only place on Earth where you can see both horizon lines at sunset. I don't believe him. We also meet this bizarre older woman who lives in Mexico City but had to leave her house for some reason she won't explain. She starts sitting too close to me and asks for my email because she's always wanted to come to New York. Her presence is not unwelcome but untrusted.

Humberto agrees to come to Preteen Gallery with me for their show London's Calling And They're Calling You Gay. We get off the train at San Cosme and wander around, passing old theaters and vine covered walls. This neighborhood, San Rafael, was the old opera district. I think of my mother the opera singer, she would think this place dirty. This neighborhood becomes my favorite.

We arrive at a stacked white building with an atrium in the center. The door is locked, so we knock. No answer. After a few moments a gentleman cracks open the door. "Lo siento...No estoy abierto…" We enter back into the night and express mutual interest in going out. Back at the hostel we meet up with some of Humberto's friends. Humberto puts on a black neoprene wetsuit for the evening. I change into a black dress with a leather jacket that I sewed a Virgin de Guadalupe sequin patch on the back. We start drinking tall boys and smoking cigarettes inside. We take a cab to a different neighborhood and immediately get some tequila shots. A nice couple takes an interest and buys two beers for us. We talk about tequila and the weather and then make our way upstairs to the live cumbia. Humberto is a far better dancer than I am, but he's not wearing creepers. Humberto unzips his neoprene wetsuit and wears it as pants with my leather jacket. We dance until our friends become bored and go outside for a cigarette. I buy a hotdog.

Two new friends have been added, Juan and Francisco, locals with a good sense of humor. We head down the block to a karaoke bar. I immediately head for the stage and sing two Selena songs which were a real hit in my mind. A light skin girl and her friends take notice of us and begin shooting dirty looks while bringing the owner onto her side. The music cuts and we're sitting in silence in the white marble bar. The light skin girl drunkenly lost her cellphone and demands everyone help her look. We exit annoyed and decide to go home. On the sidewalk outside the bar people suddenly are yelling. The light skin girl accused Juan and Francisco of stealing her cellphone and her friends start to fight them and Humberto. My biggest concern is my jacket and Virgin de Guadalupe patch. The group of fists starts moving towards me and I yell at them and shove off these idiots attacking my friends. Humberto pushes me aside and tells me to stay out of it. I continue yelling from the sidelines, adrenaline running and I start searching for this female who caused so much trouble. She's nowhere to be found and the cops show up to our block. We are told to go home, so we pile into a cab laughing and yelling about this fool who started a fight over a cellphone. Juan and Francisco tell me it started because they are dark skinned, and this happens a lot in Mexico. That light skinned girl had it out for them as soon as we walked into her club.

The night feels over and I'm ready to get into my bottom bunk. Humberto tries to convince me to sleep in his bed and I politely decline. My whole room is asleep and I see that the woman from earlier is sleeping in my top bunk. Nervous and drunk I pile my purse under my pillow and put on every article of clothing I have for security. My baby suit is filled out. I see her open one eye in her sleep and I feel like she might cut my hair off while I am asleep. I crawl into my bed, her foot drops in front of me. She swivels her ankle in smooth rounds, beckoning me to interlace my fingers with her toes. I can hear her body writhe up above me and soft moans become audible. Her sheets sound like paper. It must be my time to die, perhaps this is what that bird meant all along. I fall asleep.

SARAH ZAPATA

ELEANOR BLEIER   55

i told him it would be very easy to incarcerate me and he agreed that if he ever needs alone time he would just have to be like "officers, she is acting cray. she has a history. she's a feminist." we elaborated on this point, which seemed hilarious to both of us, for several hours. i showed him the envelope for my valuables and said I still want to get it expensively framed and we were both pretty psyched about the fact that if he locked me up just two more times i could have a triptych.

whenever i post a picture of myself (online) i think of him giving my dad a list of mental health institutions i could go to long-term, instead of for three days, as though the problem were not the prescription pills, two of which i was on for the sole purpose of dealing with the shitty relationship, or as though the problem were not the shitty relationship. i post a picture and think, oh my god, he tried to disappear me. this is also what i think about whenever i start to feel badly about talking about the situation in public.
i remember my dad clearing his throat and saying "i just want you to know he doesn't take any

responsibility for this." i was not surprised.
i am pretty shocked though—still —that he also gave my father a list of my close friends, annotated, calling one a "pushover" and saying i had a "hostile relationship" with another.
a conversation at the hospital
dad: kara, he's not who you think he is.
no, dad, he's exactly who i think he is. that's why i've been so miserable.

he, like, explicitly asked for my discretion when we started fucking…but i am getting ready to marie calloway his ass
wait. wait. wait wait wait wait. um. first of all, everyone knows if you don't want to be written about, don't date a writer. (and who isn't a writer? we all have the internet.) this goes double for dating feminist writers, who are probably committed to telling the truth about their relationships. "you're hurting me" and "ethics" and "discretion" are such obvious coverups—by self-identified feminist men—for behaviour both atrocious and foolish that they don't want exposed or theorized. it is also what jennifer doyle calls, in sex

objects, "the stubborn ignorance (and optimism) of male privilege." good luck with this one, guys. really. we were dumb, but you were dumber, and you should read the audre lorde prominently displayed on your bookshelves. we certainly have.

last night neal and ada had a really fun dinner party. a number of the guests were single straight men and some were single straight male writers, possibly for men's magazines. i took this opportunity to tell them what information i think they should be providing for their readers. this includes:

1. men should get into taxis first.
2. men should go through revolving doors first.
3. i will be significantly more impressed if a guy pays on the first date. one guy said he pays on the first two dates and i was like "that is very well-played."
4. don't talk to me about your past sex life. as one guy said, "it's a nerd move."
5. soft kisses on the cheek = gross.
we all agreed that we are sort of constitutionally built for

dating—even a misandrist like me!—in that we are or were reporters and so are generally kind of curious, plus used to spending two hours acting intimate with people we don't really know. we did not, however, all agree on the taxi issue. it was so fraught that we discussed it for like 4 hours. finally the same person who pays on the first two dates said that though it makes more sense for a man to get into a taxi first, he likes the chivalrous gesture of opening the door and, also, watching the woman. i said that i could accept this situation with a man i was interested in if i knew he was objectifying me and not merely unsophisticated.

later, neal said that he thinks the episode of "girls" that in "tiny furniture"when they have sex in a pipe evokes the definitive difference between sex in your 20s and sex in your 30s, and how in your 20s you're like "yes, totally, let's have sex in a pipe" and in your 30s you're like "it's cold, we might get caught, what about tetanus." you might want the feeling of having sex in a pipe, but without the actual pipe sex. i reiterated that also i didn't want

some guy telling me about his pipe sex. neal was like "yeah, i mean, we've all had sex with three people in a pipe."
i said that i never want to get coffee with guys, that feels like work, and neal was like "when i go to meetings i'm like, 'hey, you guys, i've got vodka in my bag'" and i started laughing.

Oh my god, boyfriend just texted saying that my tweets are "bordering worrisome" and that they're a "digital cry for help." How do I deal with that?

"tell him to fuck off?"
"pls break up with him and we can have a fun summer"

There was this time a year ago when my ex-boyfriend and i were in my apartment and i was sobbing—i would like to note i'm pretty sure that he sobbed first—and was like "i never thought i would feel like this again." this is true. i hadn't been depressed in 15 years. no therapy, no medication, mostly getting flown to las vegas on a private jet for a private celine dion

show and laughing with my then-boyfriend while watching paris hilton dance on tables at some party before she was famous and being an editor at the times and getting into a phd program.

the scariest thing that has ever happened to me—way scarier than the actual hospitalization—was being depressed after being not-depressed.

what really fucking sucked was that my ex-boyfriend would use his knowledge of the situation as a way to downplay his own shitty behaviour. it wasn't that he was an asshole for not bothering to take three hours of his life and move all of his ex-girfriends' stuff into a closet or for endlessly promising me he would go on vacation, have dinner with my friends, go to the doctor and deal with all of his medical issues; the reason i was upset was that I had a history of depression.

like, okay. but i hadn't been depressed for fifteen years. i mean, if you want to play that game, fifteen years ago he was an insecure nerd on the bowling team. (also i saw him cry all the time, and

59

also punch a wall once, and i didn't
blame it on anything. i was just like,
"wow, this fight is getting major.")
of course, when my father had to
embark on his rescue
mission—one patriarchy traded for
another—he didn't ask questions
or blame me for anything. he said
that during the brief moment when
[redacted] and i were going to get
back together he had told his wife
"this is the worst thing that could
possibly happen but i will support
her no matter what." but he also
said something that i can't even
remember that was like "well, we
know how it can be for you."
sure. let's end with a quote from
aliza again: "i don't believe in crazy
women. i only believe in bad
men."

I BOUGHT MYSELF ROSES ON
THE DAY I DECIDED TO STOP BEING
SCARED OF YOU
WHITE ROSES
THEY WERE ON SALE FOR
$4.99 PLUS TAX
I SMILED ON THE WAY
BACK TO MY CAR
IT WAS SUNNY THAT DAY

I DYED MY HAIR BLACK AND
PAINTED MY NAILS RED
YOU NOTICED AND
CALLED ME A LITTLE BITCH
AS IF I DID IT TO VEX YOU

I BOUGHT MYSELF ROSES
TWO OTHER TIMES THAT SUMMER
EACH PETAL REPLACING A FEAR
THEY'RE HANGING IN MY
NEW BEDROOM WHERE
THERE IS NO MEMORY OF YOU

ALISON RHEA   61

i'm already hungry. i've been thinking about that big carton of blackberries i bought yesterday. i wish i had a really beautiful pink or green colored glass bowl to put them in, sprinkle salt on top (not too much salt), eat them with my hands even though the berries stain my fingertips. dylan should be home soon. he gets off work around 4:30. on days like today where i don't really accomplish anything, or get out of the room even, i feel like a bored housewife awaiting her dear to come home from work. i am not that. but. somedays i feel like that. somedays i just don't feel right when he's not around. something's missing, whether it be my energy or his energy or maybe i'm just bored and afraid of talking to other people when i'm alone. i still feel very vulnerable. all the time. it's the house i think. i love this house but every once in a while i feel like an unwanted inhabitant rather than it be my place of living or my home. i just really hate the afternoon and maybe that's my issue. it doesn't really matter, because those blackberries are still sitting in the fridge. my fridge. in my house. where i am listening to Sioux and the Banshees while sitting on the bed i made where i sleep in my room in my house. where Peaches is napping at the foot of this bed and getting mad when i stop petting her.

do you ever feel scared of losing everything all at once

imagine a house fire where your family dies or

a terrible car crash

or maybe your credit card was declined at the grocery store while buying fruit and you're racking up debt daily and you just found out you have an std and your boyfriend is cheating on you and someone slashed all the tires on your car and your dog died and your father disowned you for being queer

all in a week
or a day

wouldn't that suck

the hair ties around my wrists leave imprints and make my hands sore

i need to take better care of my bones
and liver

ALISON RHEA

YOU DON'T MEET NICE GIRLS IN COPY SHOPS

for girls (and others, but mostly girls) who write zines

1. don't date anyone who requests you be silent. not even if they do it politely. not even if they only hint at it.

2. write about everyone and everything in your zine, everyone and everything that's important to you. write about the mix tape your first love made you. write about bike rides to the lake; about getting drunk and ripping your stockings. write about the night the moon was the same color as the strawberry-kiwi Mad Dog 20/20 you were drinking, which also happened to be the same color as the hair of the girl you had a crush on at the time. write about everyone you've ever fucked and everyone you've ever loved. write about your traumas, your scars, protests and arrests and abortions. write about your favorite dress, your favorite hoodie, your favorite pair of shoes. make your zine a confessional. make it so personal other people feel a little guilty for reading it, like they've stolen your secret diary.

3. or don't. write surreal tales about murder and circus freaks and mermaids. write poems about magicians and motels. put disclaimers in your zine: *this is fiction*. don't tell anyone that the stories are closer to reality than they might think.

4. change everyone's names. give them new names that represent who they are deep-down: Dark Eyes. Calloused Hands. The Moth Boy. Barefoot and Beautiful. Evan Williams. when they read it, they'll know who they are. if they don't know, they'll ask you. don't tell them.

5. when your ex-lover comes to you and says: *I can't believe you wrote about me that way. I can't believe you're letting strangers read about our history*, say: *I told you*

from the start you should never fuck a zine-writing girl, but you thought I was joking.

6. when your current lover comes to you and says: *how come you never write about me in your zine?*, say: because *I can't ever write about relationships 'til they're over.* don't say: *that means I'll never be able to write about you*, because you know - the fact that they asked that question means it will be over sooner rather than later.

7. when the person you have a crush on reads your zine and stops calling you, think: *good riddance. if they couldn't handle that, I'm better off without them.* try not to cry.

8. when your mother wants to read your zines to see if there are any 'lesbian undertones,' only give her the ones about boys. say: *this is all of them.* she will then believe you're straight, and never ask about your zines again.

9. when your girlfriend reads your zine and says: *all you ever write about is punk rock and crushes and road trips. where's all the political stuff? I guess you're not very committed to the cause.*, casually gesture toward your anarchy symbol tattoo, so she remembers that you were at least committed enough to get it permanently etched into your flesh. then, take her to a punk rock show. if she sees how much the music means to you, she'll understand.

10. when that same girlfriend reads a different issue of your zine, reads about one of those road trips you so often go on, and gets mad because you ate a burger in a roadside diner and therefore aren't a pure vegan like she is, dump her. then go out to a diner, eat a bacon cheeseburger, laugh about it. then feel sick to your stomach. try not to cry.

11. when your boyfriend reads an issue of your zine that's more overtly political than usual and scoffs at you, saying: *you're so naive. I can't believe you think anarchism would ever work in the real world.*, start singing "Only Anarchists Are Pretty." when he rolls his eyes, spit coffee in his face.

12. when your boyfriend gets jealous because you write so much about your former lovers, and tells you he's afraid you'd rather be with one of them, reassure him that the past is just a good story, and that you're very happy being with him. when he

64

tallies in his head the number of past lovers you've written about, decides it's too many, and calls you a slut - leave him. take all the beer in the fridge with you.

13. when your best friend (and sometimes-lover) reads your zine - an issue that you've stated is fiction - and comes to you asking which stories are fiction and which stories really happened, say: *they're stories*. when they keep pestering you about it, do not yell. say: *they're STORIES*. decide that someone who can't accept the blurred line between fact and fiction without explanation isn't worthy of being your best friend, or your lover.

14. when you're doing a zine reading and your other best friend - the one you spend so much time with that everyone thinks you're secretly dating - says: *read a story with me in it*, laugh, say: *which one?*

15. finish your next issue. even if you're terrified. even if it's the most personal one you've written in years. finish it. even if you fear your honesty will get you in trouble - an honest girl is always in trouble. if you're afraid that the people you're writing about will guess at their pseudonyms and get angry about the stories you're telling, write a disclaimer. state it simply: *you're so vain, you probably think this zine is about you. it's not*. finish it. stay up all night, if you have to. drink coffee 'til your hands shake. stare at the computer screen or the blank page 'til you can't see straight. finish it, if it's the last zine you do.

16. don't date anyone who demands your silence. don't date anyone who demands. don't date anyone.

just write.

MAYBE I STARTED TO HARM MYSELF IN HOPES THAT
THE PAIN WOULD SOMEHOW TRANSFER TO YOU
I TEAR AT THE SKIN AROUND MY NAILS AND THEY
RIP AND BLEED AND I SHED NO TEARS
MY KNEES BRUISE EASILY AND
I LAUGH AT THE THOUGHT
YOUR NAME IS VINEGAR
ANDYOUR MEMORY IS SHIT
THE SCARS ON MY LEG
DON'T KNOW THE DIFFERENCE

after all this time i still despise the way you looked at me
the pit of my stomach fills heavy with bricks and stone and scum and
mold
there was an innocence that you stole from me and
once i realized it would never be returned i
gathered the bricks in the pit and i started to build what is now only
my own
a sanctuary within myself
a do not disturb sign hanging
from the entrance

It's Time For White Feminists To Stop Talking About Solidarity And Start Acting

Kesiena Boom

I wasn't always a feminist, let alone one with a politicised pride in my Blackness. My first forays into feminism, through the work of women such as Kate Millett and Andrea Dworkin left me starved of any meaningful understanding of my life experiences. I feasted on their anger and zeal, but their messages didn't nourish me. Where was the representation of my life as a Black, mixed-race lesbian? Where was I to find solace and solidarity and an understanding of my existence and the oppressions unique to my position at the intersection of woman, lesbian and Black?

The feminist community currently has a basic understanding of what intersectionality means, in no small part due to the internet and the rise of online feminist activism. However, only those of us who have known the fear of slipping through the cracks can properly articulate the relief that the growing influence of this theory of oppression holds. Coined by Black feminist and legal scholar, Kimberlé Crenshaw in 1989 (following previous similar iterations by the Combahee River Collective) 'intersectionality' gives us the framework to understand the multiplicity of lived experience. It gave me insight into why my womanhood felt so different from that of my white friends and allowed me to understand the implications of being the Other on a structural level. I was able to understand that maybe some of my experiences hadn't been shaped wholly by my actions but by forces of hierarchy way outside of my control. The words of bell hooks, Patricia Hill Collins, Kimberlé Crenshaw, Barbara Smith, Audre Lorde and other Black feminist women have been instrumental to the formation of modern feminism. They are our unseen and unsung mothers.

What does it mean to me, a permanently angry brown dyke, when mainstream white feminism fights for the right to be 'sexy' and unthreatening to men and urges us to quell our fury? It persuades us to be passive, pale dolls and to dress our struggle for liberation in quiet positivity, suspenders and sex tips. Black women, such as myself, don't have the luxury of the pacifism and politeness found in today's white feminism. We must use violence, both physically and in the vehemence of our words, because we are more desperate. People of colour are over 10% more likely to face physical harassment in public than white citizens. This is true of my experiences. Once as I waited in line at a shop in Brighton the man in front of me turned around and started talking to me. When I didn't respond in a suitably enthusiastic manner, he reached out and grabbed my breast without shame. I hit his hand away, seething with rage at his audacity. I could run out of breath listing the numerous times men have grabbed my ass, my afro, my waist. I am sick of having to physically defend myself from strangers who violate the bounds of my personal space. In the past my white feminist acquaintances have been quick to admonish me for resorting to violence, even after seeing the marks left on my body by men and hearing about the way I have been repeatedly targeted. A white friend once told me he noticed that when he went out with me and my other women of colour friends, we faced noticeably more aggressive and sexualised harassment than that of his white friends. Pacifism comes from a place of privilege, as Veena Cabreros-Sud says in my all-time favourite feminist quote:

"Most white feminists look at me disdainfully when I recount some of my choice violent moments. They are appalled, morally repelled by this unbecoming behavior. One even giggled, holding her breastbone ever so lightly and saying she's not the violent type, blah blah blah. The messages are, 1.) I'm educated and you're not, 2.) I'm upper class and you're not, 3.) I'm a feminist and you're not (since her brand of feminism is equated with nonviolent moon-to-uterus symbiosis). My "men" can do the fighting, but I, gentle maiden, shan't; the new feminism remaking a generation in the image of the suburban, wealthy, sophisticated, genetically genteel. No one protected me when a loved one cracked my head on a public street one night, not even the college educated Upper West Side white women strolling by pretending not to notice. I don't like getting hit either, but what are you gonna do when someone grabs your tits? Meekly whisper you won't stoop to your attacker's level? And what level is that exactly? If that's the way "women" react, how do we classify the elderly Filipinas on a subway train who, when Joe Dickwad grabbed my ass, congratulated me for whacking him as hard as I could, screaming obscenities, and chasing him — to his utter shock and dismay — through the station? They were the few who seemed to acknowledge, respect, and allow for "aggressive" forms of resistance instead of strapping on moral straightjackets for the nineties

which we "women" must squeeze into. If that's a woman, I'm not one. I am an animal who eats, sleeps, fucks, and fights voraciously – I assume a "good" woman does it gently and in the missionary position only."

We have less to lose and more to gain than white women. We are more likely to be unemployed, are more likely to go to prison, and struggle to see truthful reflections of ourselves onscreen and in print. If we soothe men with one hand and fix our hair with the other, like popular exclusionary feminism tells us to, then which fist is left to smash the system that chokes us? There is no room in the language of liberal feminism and its conservatism for the blood and bile that is spilt from those of us who stray from the normative. In fact we, as brown women, as angry women, as women loving women are admonished by our smoother, safer, softer sisters for holding the fight back with the suffocating scent of our lavender menace and the stings of our fists.

White, rich, straight, cisgender women such as Lena Dunham and Lily Allen control the mainstream feminist discourse (even whilst shirking the feminist label in the case of the latter) and form the wider public opinion on the movement, as they are afforded the coverage to bring their ideas to the masses. Rhiannon Lucy Coslett and Holly Baxter of *The Vagenda* have half the talent and insight of Mia Mckenzie of Black Girl Dangerous, the website that amplifies the voices of queer and trans feminists of colour yet it is they who have recently had a major book published and regular columns in *The Guardian* and the *New Statesman*. The aforementioned white women don't use their privileged platform to uplift the sisters below them. Instead they dig their heels into our shoulders, stride across the bridges we call our backs, without so much as a glance down. They ignore women of colours' righteous fury at the double bind we face under white supremacist patriarchy.

Time and time again we see white feminists such as Caitlin Moran and Julie Burchill enact their brand of selfish individualistic feminism upon us. We see them proclaim that they 'literally couldn't give a shit' about their sisters of colours' right to media representation, in the case of Moran, whose best-selling book *How To Be A Woman* repeatedly uses the t slur as well as being cissexist and biologically essentialist throughout. Or we see them write odes to racist thought - Burchill's *Damaged Gods* talks about the barbarity and backwardness of men of colour, yet she is still hailed as a progressive feminist voice, her views are legitimised by the prominent platform she is given as the go to outspoken feminist in the English media. This is a position she has held for decades despite publishing multiple transphobic tirades, most notably a horrifically transmisogynistic piece in the Observer in 2013 which denigrated trans women in ways too vile to repeat. Flavia Dzodan, Latina feminist and originator of the oft-quoted line, "My feminism will be intersectional or it will be bullshit!", wrote an entire article about the numerous high profile white feminists (such as Sarah Ditum, noted Guardian journalist) who have rubbished intersectionality. It describes how they are swathing their discomfort with something not wholly made for them in accusations of complexity and alienation — all in one simple concept about the actuality of our multi-faceted lives?! We cannot and will not stand for this deliberate destruction of Black women's intellectual labour.

To be feminist is to be aware of our interconnected struggle as women, but to also see that not every struggle is our own. Use your voice as a privileged white woman to shout down racism wherever you see it. Be thankful that you will never know the sickening lurch that sways through your blood when your humanity is denounced and denied because of your race by women who profess to care about all women's liberation. The title feminist is to be taken up by women who have moved beyond a selfish view of one's relationship to society, an outlook that is nurtured and encouraged by the neo-liberal matrix we find ourselves struggling to survive in. It is difficult to throw off no doubt, but we can and we must. In her speech "The Transformation of Silence Into Language and Action," Audre Lorde spoke of how she was doing her work to dismantle the binds of this sick sad world and questioned her sisters, '…are you doing yours?'

I once wrote a Facebook status explaining how sick and tired I am of asking white people to stop wearing bindis and fashioning their hair into the mess that they have the audacity to call dreadlocks. Predictably, it didn't end well. I explained that I can't abide the blatant and flagrant cultural appropriation of symbols that are dear to people of colour. It's simply not fair that people of colour's own cultural markers mark them out as 'backwards', 'unclean' or 'unprofessional' while white people don the same things and are lauded for their (stolen) creativity and uniqueness. White women who have sat by my side in feminist meetings, who I was once proud to call my sisters, rushed to shout me down and accuse me of stirring hatred and racism and it then dissolved into personal attacks on my character. The thing that really struck me was their repeated affirmations that they cared deeply about tackling racism and wanted to work together to end it. Well to them I say: listen the hell up when a woman of colour calls you out! I was literally giving them an easy way to chip a little bit of racism away from the world but their cognitive dissonance is so strong that they can say we will fight racism with one side of their mind whilst perpetuating it with the other. This is how whiteness operates; it is insidious and sly. It lets white women feel that they have the coolness and collectedness of reasoned, dispassionate logic on their side and thus they reign righteous over women of colour's understandable anger and frustrations.

I once made the mistake of falling for a 'feminist' white girl who would get angry at me for daring to call out the racism and misogynoir of a mutual male friend, though of course she would never admit that she might hold racist thoughts herself via her tone-policing and what I came to see as her fetishistic view of me and other Black people. This is the reality of our white supremacist society, and by extension the feminism of white women who allow it to permeate them without critical reflection.

Then there are those white women who steal the language Black women have created to articulate our situations. They will declare themselves 'intersectional feminists,' and as they take this word as their own, they soften its edges and declare themselves absolved of their whiteness. Stop paying superficial lip service to intersectionality, white feminists. It is insulting and strips the power from one of the most important concepts in the politics of gender liberation. If you can't take a stand against racism you have no business calling yourself intersectional for feminist brownie points. I can't listen to a white feminist who coos about her love of bell hooks but dismisses the words of a woman of colour she knows on the subject of race.

73

When will white feminists take collective responsibility for educating themselves? When will they understand the power at play that sings in their skins? We don't exist in a vacuum and women of colour don't exist to hold their hands and explain in painful detail why their behaviour continues to hurt us. Intersectional feminist politics are not for white women to co-opt as their own. It is explicitly a theory that was formed from the mind of a Black woman, Kimberlé Crenshaw, to explain Black women's situations under the law. They could not sue for discriminatory practises against them as Black women, but rather simply as women or Black, which glossed over the actuality of their situations. I cannot speak for every Black woman, and I would never profess to. We are not a monolith. But I think we ought to stand wary of a white woman who calls herself intersectional. You won't listen to us and you will exclude us from your movement but you will take the ideas you like? It is far more impressive and sisterly to me to see white women *acting* in a way that reflects their acknowledgement of racialised differences in womanhood. I want to see them reach a point where they are critical of the feminist action they take and weed out the racism that seeps through their organising and the feminist media they consume. I want to see white feminists understand why they can't use racist narratives, such as those that surround the Western view of Muslim women who choose to wear hijab, to fight sexism. They must understand that they are not the default. That white is not synonymous with womanhood. We, as women of colour, are women too. We are their sisters. I long for the day that they call out and collect their fellow white people instead of letting women of colour do it time and time again at the expense of our mental and physical health. That is sisterhood. That is selflessness; and it is precious.

For women of colour intersectional thinking is a reflex to us. We cannot divorce our race from our womanhood. I cannot tease apart my lesbian identity from my gender or from my Blackness. I am all of me, all of the time. When white feminists perpetuate a weak form of feminism that implies I ought to choose between the many facets of myself, all women are betrayed. What is feminism when it merely affords a privileged few women the impunity to act just as the white men around them? That is not my liberation. White women must stand beside, not in front of us and force themselves to think about who exactly their feminism is fighting for.

74

TRY HYPNOSIS

THE
THING FROM
THE CRYPT

B

previous page: DANA GOLDSTEIN
JANE CHARDIET

how dare you Bret Michaels

a man made me cry today!!!!! a man with leathery skin and callousy hands. there are people who use the words LOVE and HEART and FEELINGS and SEXY about a man who has mentioned his penis 15 times in the last hour

take a drink every time they say the word AROUSED

i haven't seen a girl furrow her brow like that or yell like that since i was in 6th grade i learned what it was like to really sweat and not know what to say and have boys watch while girls tear each other apart with their eyes

yaknow I'm really pissed off I'm pissed off that you would mess with my emotions you make me feel like some kind of freak I'm pissed off that you would lie to me I just want to know how you really feel it doesn't matter what the other girls think i want to know that you're here for me I'm pissed off I want two girlfriends

boys watch and they laugh boys watch and they cheer I watch and I can't imagine doing anything but try to be her friend do you like Pantera? do you want to talk about Pantera? let's go to the bathroom and talk about how much we like Pantera

take a drink every time they say something mean about breasts

girls smile when they're mad this is real life I've never had a girl clap her hands at me while she yelled but this is real life I CAN'T BE FRIENDS WITH GIRLS breaks my heart we're pinned against each other we pin each other down we put each other down

is this a fight? are we fighting? I'm so sad this is real life

I've slept on a lot of couches in the past year and every time I lay down in a cold place I cry and it's not because it's a cold place but because people exchange a moment of intimacy that doesn't get talked about for six months

take a drink every time they say they care about your personality

I don't want to share you

I watched this relationship fall apart in six months I watched this relationship fall apart in twelve hours this relationship was based on a lot of things that required decisions there was always a decision to make and who can say what the right one is?? who can say I just had to say good bye to someone could you smile for me anyway could you smile for the camera could you smile while I walk away

take a drink every time they make you cry

I don't care what America thinks of me I don't care what Florida thinks of me I don't care what you think of me I don't care what I think of me I don't care what she thinks of me I don't care

take a drink every time

The Wardrobe Department

Pink
I am in the changing room of one of my favourite vintage shops trying on a 1940's pink silk ball gown. It doesn't have proper straps but I'm certain it can be altered to fit.

Lavender
I don't have anything lavender in my wardrobe at the moment but it is my favourite colour for eye shadows and nail polish.

Blue
When I wear blue, whether as a cardigan or on my eyelids - I think of the sky and the ocean and feel a sense of the wide open.

Red
"The Scarlet Woman"
Who is anyone to say who has transgressed?
It's the colour of everyone's blood. Animals too.

Leopard print
When I wear the markings of big cats I feel timid and powerful.

TO EQUATE MONEY WITH GUTS

Intimacy lasts for 30 mins at most as a reassurance
Is probably the bleakest thing I have ever heard
None of you have any idea.

I don't know why I screenshot your cock
Because I am not brave
Maybe because there is no outside and because everything looks the
same.

I am sick of hearing about women
And their bodies and their work
And their care.

Things are worse for smiling

I don't want to preform anything
I want to be carried home on the base of your shoe.

ONE

"In the current period, *tact* should be considered the cardinal revolutionary virtue, and not abstract radicality--and by 'tact' we mean the art of nurturing revolutionary becomings."
-- To Our Friends, The Invisible Committee

There's a billboard on Broad Street that says: "10 Transgender Women have been murdered so far in 2015." It was a response to a 21 year old transgender woman, Penny Proud, who was killed earlier this year here. You know about that, Sophie? It's paramount that this billboard is geographically sandwiched between Orleans Parish Prison and the overpass where its eye-level to the people driving to work each morning and where the city's infrastructure hides its deceptively drab violence. The billboard is accessible and friendly, with an illustration of Penny smiling. This is a strategic move by BreakOUT!, the organization that raised money to put the billboard up not as a peaceful response but to gain deliberate control over media coverage when talking about transgender youth. Its physical presence is staking claim. Its intended friendliness, unlike other billboards that mean to shock (like anti-abortion ads often do), humanizes the lives of these women and takes on the difficult task of opening up the conversation for any onlooker who can be impacted, holding any of us accountable.

For those of us who have it: dare to flare in the pastoral; subvert with charm and grace.

TWO

When my family moved here from the Philippines, my mother would take us to a low cost dental clinic off of US Highway 19. It was right next to a bright blue Entenmann's Bakery Outlet building. She took us to the dentist all the time because we never went to the dentist in the Philippines. No one really had insurance over there and it was difficult to find government assistance when there wasn't such a thing to begin with. Anyway, US-19 was notoriously named one of the most dangerous roads in Florida by Readers Digest or Dateline or any other reputable source like that. I mention it because the highway ran right through my hometown of Port Richey, Florida where I was surrounded by poor people, poorer people than me, and mostly white. I make that distinction because it's important for me to make that distinction. We were poor and people of color but we were nowhere near as poor as some of the white people I knew or the white people that lived in trailers. There were people of color there too who were poorer and who lived in trailers as well.

I only say these things because if you grow up off of US-19, you may likely fuck some racists. Before going to college, you may have *only* fucked racists. It may not even be a big deal except for that you're Filipino and the only other pinays you know are your mom and your sister. I'm talking like… Guy Harvey wearin' ass, chewin' ass racists. A South African you met at a friend's house party racist. Sons of veterans' sons who quoted inspiring G.I. rape advice racists. Fetishists racists. Emo and punk racists which made it all the more confusing racists. Subtle racist boyfriends that say things like "there are so many Filipina nurses because they're nurturing and like to serve."

I didn't know what racism and misogyny truly meant when I was experiencing it the most, around the ages of 12-22. In my memory bank, both things were like crusty inside slippers or a sunbleached American flag decal faded to a black and clear yellow--they exist in their old yet tangible state whether I signify them or not.

Both things were steeped in my sexual experience moving through this harsh landscape, a kind of kink blossoming. I was never violently abused--never *too* bad--which I consider a privilege and one I am grateful for because a kink can just be a kink and stay there most days. Don't laugh but I can look at someone, say, Riff Raff and appreciate him, want to be him, want to be as free and dead inside, be aroused by him, and hate that he exists. What does that say about me? Not much, I hope. Except for maybe that I'm an apologist, an open participant in the patriarchal system, that I see through the oppressor's eyes a bit too clearly? Maybe so but I sincerely hope that radicals don't get it twisted: I know the side I'm on and I know what my enemy is but it's not just some poor white depressive snorting pills in his brother's house. He cannot escape his geographic experience inasmuch as I couldn't when I was younger. My estranged twin nieces, living in a more backwoods part of Florida than I grew up in, can't escape their geography either. They are just there. Moving through life with more multiplicities in their identities than they can name.

THREE

A month ago, the U.S. Marine charged with killing Jennifer Laude, a transgender woman, finally confessed to choking her in a hotel room near his naval base in the Philippines. This case caught wider stateside attention here because the U.S. just entered an agreement with the Philippines in April to post more American military personnel in exchange for a stronger defense backing for the archipelago's disputed territories with China.

This is a clear example of the United States as a geopolitical power imposing its lasting effect and military control on the Philippines - on its ports and access points - on its people - on its trans demographic (the latter already having to struggle for civil rights within its own native population.) The trans rights movement has been garnering political success here in pockets of America. Movements that represent a single common cause have a tendency to vary in success rate and resource distribution depending on factors, including geography. They start in territories that have the most

88

access to capital and trickle ever so slowly to places like New Orleans and to a global scale, to developing countries like the Philippines. I'm neither trans nor a pinoy citizen and again, I make that distinction because it's important that I make that distinction. It hit me hard anyway to witness a U.S. Marine committing a hate crime on a trans woman could have had military protection, or worse, impunity. It is painful enough to read the American soldier, the American and Filipino media, and even Jennifer's family lawyer refer to her as a man and not as the gender she designated herself, further flattening and silencing her dynamism. Could Jennifer Laude, the subaltern in this space, ever truly speak?

Anxiety makes a list

In grade school when I took to heart all the fear mongering of the Stranger
and a man ran after me trying to return my scarf that had fallen in the snow
and I peed my snowpants.

In junior high canvassing for some ridiculous school sponsored charity
on Academy street with Emily Adkins-Taylor clipboards in hand
and a man approaches us asking if we are old enough for sex
and we run back home and call the police
"Did he touch you?" they ask.

My first sentence at age two coming down from a roof was
DIRTY JESUS DOG FACED MOTHER FUCKING PIG

In the middle of the kitchen floor Mother and I are sitting in a puddle of urine
I am four and she is trying to remove a three inch long sliver from my hand
Thick hardwood

Earlier between the evergreens with all the kids from the Western University
family housing loop, discussion that morning was the proposed burning of
one of the twins
Ring leader proclaiming that since there were two of them, one could easily
be sacrificed.
Scrawny long blonde matching girls sob uncontrollably
as I flee the grove
running as fast past the dark tall wood fence
a massive wooden shard impales itself in my hand
JESUS DOG FACED MOTHER FUCKING PIG

In high school the acute phobia of splinters morphs into fetishistic pleasure
at their removal
working carpentry with Father

90

"You should really just let that fester" he says
"It'll puss right out"

Once he nailed his hand to the stud of a wall with the nail gun.
Amidst DOG FACED JESUS CHRIST ON THE CROSS jokes I cut the head
off so that he can pull his hand out of the nail
its metal surface passing through tissue
blood pouring down
thats when we all went a little woozy
luckily it missed bone so he just duct taped it up and we kept on working.

In the walk-in closet when she duct taped a condomed banana down onto the
hardwood floor….

On the beach outside the all inclusive family resort in Cuba, where they were
all on holiday in memory of Grandma whose dying wish has been no funeral
but this drunken trip together, where in the night she is on her knees in the
sand sucking the cock of a french teenager who won't stop singing the refrain
from Madonna's Holiday.

In the foyer of other Grandmother's penthouse apartment, she is house
sitting and
he is going down on her
on a turkish runner under the mirror
they have been together a year
but have never peneratedly fucked
he is either gay or terrified of her potential HIV positive status
from that year she lived with that man in Africa
married now, so maybe the latter?

On the Extraterrestrial Highway, with another man, bypassing Reno
on the way to Vegas via his Grandmother's Montana ranch

on a large section of unmarked open pasture road
it is night, foggy, low on gas
cows continually cross, does he have Dark Side of the Moon on?
lone old Cadillacs pass
with serial killers inside waiting for us up ahead
to run out of gas.

Travel and new man and I am constipated; haven't shat in days
first time in desert proper, but paralyzed by every horror movie scene I have never seen
 no tv as a child….
convinced I am either gonna be serial killed, alien abducted or crash into a cow
"Stop the car" I say and feebly "Need to pee"
 as I can feel the shit literally being scared right out of me
"I am going to need that box of Kleenex"

Later that roadtrip Anxiety has a total collapse in some town with Springs in its name
we finally get to Sante Fe and I buy a ridiculous turquoise wide brim felted hat
there are lots of nude photographs taken in the shower that has a stain glass window
we are still using film
we are together five years
until I make out with a werewolf man
in a pool in Miami
at the Art Fair.

On the computer I didn't mean to start watching Africa's Next Top Model
snake eating its tail that is the internet
willowy women with amazing bone structure are on location to save the
children from the perils of periods with the help of their sponsor Proctor and
Gamble; PG, as host Oluchi Onweagba calls them
 "OK kids. Lets all thank PG for keeping girls in school" she exclaims to a

92

packed auditorium of bewildered kids receiving boxes of Kotex pads from aspiring models in stilettoes

Without pads girls in the South African township are forced to stay home from school when bleeding.

For the camera, the children chant THANK YOU PG FOR KEEPING GIRLS IN SCHOOL! THANK YOU PG FOR KEEPING GIRLS IN SCHOOL!

I don't remember bleeding much when I was in Botswana
likely a result of the expired black market birth control I was taking
also the voodoo witchcraft crack eating break with reality convinced i would die of AIDS situation
seems to overshadow memories of menstruation

In Otse in the little brick house with its tin roof it is night
the man fucking me says
"YOU that side will never understand this place."

EYETOOTH

MY BEST FRIEND'S A BUTCHER AND HE HAS 16 KNIVES.
HE CONSTANTLY CARRIES THEM AROUND
BECAUSE THEY'RE HIS ONLY TRUSTWORTHY COMPANIONS...
YOU KNOW, JUST IN CASE HE NEEDS TO CUT YOU UP INTO
10 MILLION TED BUNDY BITE SIZE PIECES.
HE COULD DO IT.
AND I DON'T DOUBT THAT HE'S DONE IT BEFORE.
HE'S GOT TEETH AS SHARP AS 'EM
AND A HAGGARD JAWLINE JUST TO PROVE IT;
CONTAINING RIBALD CONFESSIONS,
RIBCAGING HIS OBSCENE ULUTATIONS --
FRANKLY, IT MAKES HIM ALL THE MORE ECLECTIC.
IS IT FATE SCHEMING?
HIS BOWLEGS ASTRADDLE THE MECHANICAL BULL AT THE BAR,
HE FEARLESSLY TELLS ME OF HIS LIBIDREAMS
FROM ALL THE WAY ACROSS THE RING.
HIS BRAZENLY BURLESQUE BABBLES CONFESS:
"IT WAS A PUSSY AS DELICATE AS PANSIES
WITH LIPS LIKE PETALS DRIPPING FROM A FRESH RAIN --
IT'S A SHAME I CAN ONLY TASTE IT
IN MY DREAMS."
MISTAKES WERE MADE.
WE PARTED WAYS.
AS NEON LIGHTS WOULD SHATTER HIS EGO,
HE'D RELAPSE,
REPLICATING THE DEMON THAT HE ONCE WAS.
HE FOUND HIS LOLITA AND SNATCHED HER.
SHE WHIMPERED IN HIS MEAT GRINDER MAN'S GRIP,
AND HE SAID, "YOU KNOW HOW SOME PEOPLE WEAR
THOSE DUMBASS SHARK TOOTHS AROUND THEIR NECKS?
IMMA YANK YOUR EYES OUT YOUR SOCKETS
AND WEAR 'EM JUST LIKE THAT, HONEY.
I DON'T WANNA FALL IN LOVE WITH YOU,

I JUST WANNA SLICE YOUR PUNY ASS IN TWO."
AND SO HE DID.
BALLISTIC CANNIBAL ROLAND FOUND HIS FLOWER
AND HE BELLIGERENTLY ATE HER RIGHT UP, TOO.
DRIP BY BLOODY DRIP.
PIECE BY TED BUNDY PIECE.
SUCKLE SAD GIRLS NEVER TASTED SO SWEET.

kids or plants

I spend my time thinking about these topics: intimacy and my lack therein.

Last night for the first time in my 38 years it was a woman - not a man - who led me to my room and kissed me, took off my shorts and fingered me. I developed a rash - in media res, and when we came out of my room there was a small bruise under my right eye. Why does every experience have to mark me? I am not one who opens herself up for casual visual confirmation of her whims. And yet my skin - it records everything and heals so slowly.

I am not in control.

I like to be guarded and alone. I preferred this even as a child. Seeing a person on a regular basis - once per week - is more of a commitment than I want. I make this seem wrong to me, because doesn't it prevent me from enjoying a broader range of emotional response? I refuse many an opportunity for new discomfort. Everything looks the same to me. I am inside, not outside.

"You can be courageous and afraid at the same time." "If everyone waited until they were ready to change, no one would ever change." "Alcohol is not comfort food. And a drinking habit is not a harmless teddy bear." I know, and yet I constantly need the messaging.

People act in ways that force your response. Most times you will not be asked for your consent. How you respond is how you will later think about yourself. When cornered call to mind your favorite internet presence or literary figure and act accordingly. You can become a self you love by aping those you admire. Eventually those qualities will become yours because there is no way you can habitually copy without transmogrifying the essentials into your own special material body.

Do not get plastic surgery.

I'm honest on my blog but evasive in real life. I will reconcile the differences or not. Hidden provocations provide respite. I do not appreciate the small town experience. Familiarity pins me down and leaves me hopeless. Anonymity in public spaces provides the opportunity to craft a self that dwells in the immediate present. I am this right now. You don't know me; you can't refute.

PERPETUALLY SPILLING
CONSTANTLY COPING

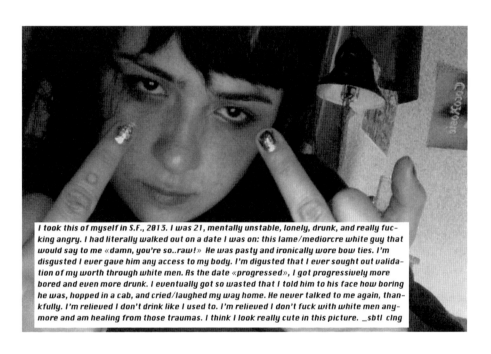

I took this of myself in S.F., 2013. I was 21, mentally unstable, lonely, drunk, and really fuc-king angry. I had literally walked out on a date I was on: this lame/mediorcre white guy that would say to me «damn, you're so..raw!» He was pasty and ironically wore bow ties. I'm disgusted I ever gave him any access to my body. I'm digusted that I ever sought out valida-tion of my worth through white men. As the date «progressed», I got progressively more bored and even more drunk. I eventually got so wasted that I told him to his face how boring he was, hopped in a cab, and cried/laughed my way home. He never talked to me again, than-kfully. I'm relieved I don't drink like I used to. I'm relieved I don't fuck with white men any-more and am healing from those traumas. I think I look really cute in this picture. _sbtl clng

SBTL CLNG

ALEXIS GROSS

MEN WILL TELL YOU
THAT THINGS YOU LOVE
DO NOT BELONG TO YOU;
SCREAMING, ORGASMS,
PUNK ROCK, LITERATURE

MEN WILL TOUCH YOUR THIGHS
AND GET THEIR HOPES UP
CRUSH THEM
AND TAKE A SIP OF GIN

YOU'RE OKAY
YOU'VE ALWAYS BEEN

SARA SUTTERLIN

Life by way of Love

Zoe tells me the reason it is so hard for women to lose the weight around our
thighs and lower bellies
is that this is our bodies' way of protecting our uterus for a future fetus.

This is our flesh building a home in which to grow new life.

Some days, she says, sipping water in the café of the Plaza Nueve de Julio,
some days, the soft billows of her flesh are graceful swoops and curves.
They cushion her, dive up and down her body with the force of ocean waves.
Other days they are mountains she cannot climb,
and she pinches at their foreignness with distrustful fingers.
I contemplate another piece of bread from the basket on the table and think
of something small, hungry and alive trying to find a home in the one-room
cell of my inner organs, their cold walls.
I feel I am deconstructing somebody's house before they have even moved
in.
It's heavy, having a body, I exhaled once to an ex-love, and he was
surprised. But I can't imagine what it would be to move throughout this world
without the constant sensation of soft flesh that seems to grow and boil as it
meets the eyes of passersby.

On our way back to the hostel we are whistled at by six men at a gas station.
Their eyes are Velcro, unstuck fiber by fiber as Zoe's long ponytail
disappears around the corner in front of me.
She hasn't gone a day since she was fourteen without this type of thing
happening, she says.
She says it makes her want to smile less.

Sometimes I feel my hipbones, how they jut out without me asking, and
remember how a boy I wanted so badly to love me told me they were hot.
His sweatpants fell all the way off me as I climbed into bed to sleep next to
him without touching all night. It was the last time we slept together.

I *love* men, but I *understand* women.

How hard it is to make our bodies feel like our own.

How Velcro fibers sting and stick as they follow you down the block.

Each one a reminder that people can take what is not theirs.

That people take what is not theirs.

And we cut down the flesh built around these homes

only to feel them given up inch by inch

We are made to produce life by way of love, and yet our bodies are turned

against us-

    for Zoe it was fourteen when her flesh began to billow

for another one of us, it was the night about a year ago when a boy decided

to take what was not his.

The four of us sit in the corner of the hostel room, all touching, hands on shoulders, heads on tender knees. We form an unbroken circle through which our power passes. We cannot give back what has been taken, but we can use these electric currents, this strong and gentle flesh, to rebuild. It's ok, we whisper, *It's ok*, and through each touch we produce life by way of love.

LOOKING AT LOOKING AT FLOWERS

one of the things that made me angriest last year
was coming across a quote by this French historian Michelet
who thought that women could learn everything they needed to by
observing a flower
i.e.
how to be silent, natural, delicate and beautiful
and this made me very angry
but what made me angrier was that
he had taken away the possibility of contemplation for me
so that if i looked at flowers
i would be submitting to this pedagogic tyranny
in which everything is turned against my subjectivity
and i'm once again forced to be immobile or compliant with a system
that has colonised flora
to instructively oppress
~
i got these flowers for my birthday
the smell is a bit potent but i like it, like a girl with her legs open
i have always pressed flowers in pages of heavy theory
while condescending boys sneer on
"i can't believe you drew lovehearts in the margins of de Certeau"
and what of it, asshole
?

i used to hate the girlness of my name

but now i'm seeing looking at flowers differently
quote "intersubjectivity"
i am so used to looking at myself and other girls as objects
that i need to practice looking at a subject that is not a man

looking at flowers refusing to reduce another to myself

looking at flowers respecting difference

looking at flowers seeing beauty that is not mine and not wanting to uproot it

looking at flowers a gaze that is not predatory or judgemental

looking at flowers a sensory mediation between itself and my body

looking at flowers intermediary props between me and other girl-subjects

looking at flowers by loving another subject, i achieve my own beauty

you looking at me looking at flowers: a gift from me to you, between us, by
us and for us, let's reclaim PETALS from the PETTY, i want us to relate extra-
syntactically, take these flowers & revel in their beauty that unravels yours
and mine, press them to your cheeks, i would hold your hands, *let your eyes
unfurl a thousand reciprocal, shimmering, subjectivities*

DAISY LAFARGE

THE WORK IS ABOUT SOMETHING LATENT
THE WORK IS ABOUT LATENCY
THE WORK IS VERY LATE, BUT STILL A SUCCESS
THE WORK IS SEEN AS IMPORTANT BY THE WRONG PEOPLE
THE WORK FEELS NO RESPONSIBILITY TO ITS SUBJECT
THE WORK WILL GO ABOUT THIS THE RIGHT WAY, OR NOT AT ALL
THE WORK RETAINS THE RIGHT TO REMAIN SILENT
THE WORK IS AWARE OF TECHNICAL DIFFICULTIES
THE WORK REQUIRES AT LEAST FIVE PEOPLE AT ANY ONE TIME
THE WORK IS YOUR DISREGARD
THE WORK IS INTEGRAL TO THE SPACE AND VICE VERSA
THE WORK DOES NOT NEED TO BE VIEWED
THE WORK WILL OFTEN SLIP IN AND OUT OF SYNCH
THE WORK IS GOING TO BE COOL FOR A GODDAMN MINUTE
THE WORK WILL BE HAPPY TO HELP
THE WORK IS OFTEN SLIPPERY
THE WORK HOLDS ALL THE CARDS
THE WORK IS SUBLIMELY ORDINARY
THE WORK IS SEMINAL
THE WORK MUST NOT BE LEFT UNATTENDED AT ANY TIME
THE WORK IS THE BACK OF YOUR EX-PARTNER'S NECK
THE WORK IS WITHOUT PHYSICAL SUBSTANCE
THE WORK, AND OTHER WORKS
THE WORK IS WITHOUT HUMOUR
THE WORK CANNOT DEFY ANY EXPECTATION
THE WORK IS WITHOUT ANY REAL GRASP ON REALITY
THE WORK IS THE SWEETEST OF ALL SORROWS
THE WORK IS A FAMILY ANECDOTE
THE WORK MAY WRONG-FOOT
THE WORK IS A ONE-LINER
THE WORK ASKS THAT YOU KINDLY WATCH YOUR STEP
THE WORK IS A FAILURE OF SORTS
THE WORK IS OMNI-REFERENTIAL
THE WORK IS BEYOND THE PALE
THE WORK IS THE THING

GRACE DENTON

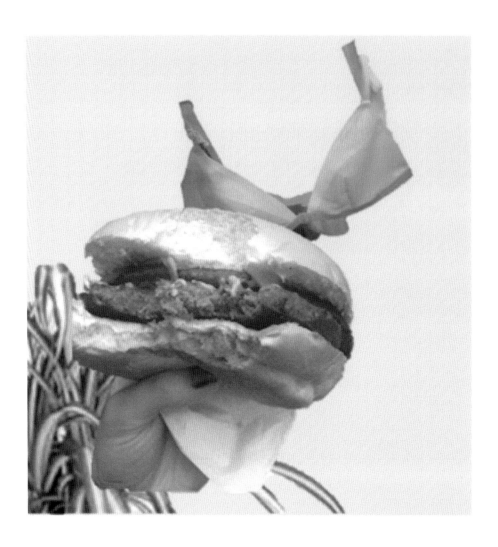

I'm making work for a screensaver residency. I'll make the images with work / life / art / balance / tiredness in mind. My work is often on the background of my phone because that's where I look all the time, and it certainly ain't in a gallery, so I may as well go with it.

Take part: receive art images to your phone / computer every month or week, DM me on Twitter (@JessicaMendham) I'd love to send you stuff.

108   *JESSICA MENDHAM*

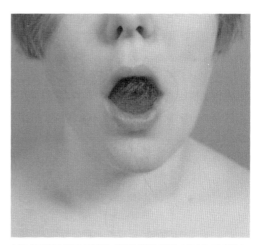

A SINGLE MISPLACED STRAND / LIKE A NEST / LIKE UNBLOCKING A DRAIN / AND I REMEMBERED LICKING YOUR CHEST / AND I REMEMBERED GET-TING A FANCY MEAL FOR FREE WHEN I FOUND A SHORT CURLED HAIR IN MY STARTER / AND WHEN THE DRY MASS HIT THE BACK OF MY THROAT I WRETCHED / YOU DON'T KNOW WHAT'S GOOD FOR YOU / THINGS IN PLACES THEY SHOULDN'T BE / LIKE EXCESS LIKE LEFTOVERS / PUTTING THINGS INSIDE OF YOU / AND WHEN YOU ARE GONE I PICK YOUR DARK COILS OF HAIR FROM THE BEDSHEETS / BREATHE IN THE SMELL OF SCALP / THESE AREN'T EVEN MY DESIRES / WHO ARE YOU TO TELL ME WHAT IS GOOD FOR ME / WHAT IS GOOD FOR ME / WHERE THE OUTSIDE MOVES TO THE INSIDE / OUTSIDES BECOME INSIDES / HOW MUCH DOES IT HAVE TO GO IN TO COUNT / TICKLE / SHE WAS MORE RIPE THAN I WITH HAIR IN HER PLACES / MY STOMACH GROWLS / WHAT I DO TO MYSELF / WHO DECIDES WHAT IS RIGHT WHEN WE DO THINGS TOGETHER / I CAN'T TELL THE DIFFERENCE BETWEEN WHAT I WANT AND WHAT YOU WANT / YOU THINK THIS IS OUT OF PLACE / A SINGLE MISPLACED STRAND / YUCK

IONA ROISIN

Silence and trading intimacies

Sylvia Plath's poem 'In Plaster' has always held particular resonance to me. It pits the inner and outer self against one another through the analogy of a body contained within a white plaster-cast at hospital.

The beautiful and impenetrable plaster cast – a social mask or persona – contains within it a less acceptable self - a body which is ugly and hairy, whom Sylvia terms 'old yellow'.

In the poem, the outer and inner self are locked in to a relationship of co-dependence and conflict. The outer shell takes its shape around the real substance of her being; it relies on her for its existence but consistently betrays her by entombing, concealing and silencing her. This inner, essential, self resentfully depends on the outer mask to survive socially, but treats it with disdain, accusing it of having a slave-like mentality, lapping up criticism and striving to meet others expectations.

When I started studying philosophy, I became particularly drawn to Berkeley's Idealism, a theory that begins with our relationship to the world as a perceiving subject and leads to the radical conclusion that we are alone with our perceptions and there is no corresponding reality.

What drew me to this theory was the image of entombment. When I taught it, I used an image of a cemented up telephone box as a thought experiment. I asked students to imagine being trapped inside, reliant on the information received down the phone line to tell them about the world outside of the cement box.

The predicament shown through this image is a solipsistic one, and not unlike the image of Sylvia Plath's plaster cast.

Although Berkeley's focus was our perception of reality and the doubt cast over the reliability of our perception of it – an extreme form of subjectivity, it too denotes a sense of containment and isolation, a mediated/indirect relationship with the world we inhabit.

What unites them is a self that is fundamentally isolated.

The difference is that Plath's imprisonment is self-imposed.

But for me, the question was one of communication. How do we communicate in a way that lets our real self out, and is it even possible? Is there a wall around us? If there is, then how do we break down the wall, with words?

Perhaps I was drawn to these images in literature and philosophy because silence has always been a personal battle for me. I've always been shy; in my last year of senior school I was basically mute. My shyness was one of the drives behind training to teach at the time – I wanted to grapple with my fear of being in the spotlight. I wanted to learn to speak.

Text, on the other hand, is a space where I've always given myself permission to speak. It's a space where the distinction between outer and inner self collapses. I write all the things I should have said.

At home I have a question bowl. I ask all visitors to contribute a few handwritten questions anonymously, and over the past few years it's become fairly full with questions ranging from the psychoanalytic to crude to hypothetical post-apocalyptic survival scenarios. But I find that it gives people a certain permission to talk differently, sometimes more intimately. Some friends have even reported back that they enjoyed the sense of embarrassment they felt at times.

Never underestimate a shy person's desire to confess their secrets!

While my own self-imposed silence is something I've grappled with most of my life, silence has also come to take on broader, even political significance to engender history, literature, minorities and the 'Other'.

I was surprised recently to read of Anais Nin's admission of being mute - *"When I was thirty I listened always to other people, and I never said a word. I was really mute. So I taught myself to talk, and I owe to writing the fact that we can talk together now."* In 'A Woman Speaks' Nin uses a similar analogy to Plath, in describing the way we might entomb ourselves for our own protection. The essential self on the inside then withers as a consequence of this compromise. She speaks of trying to give up the 'persona' – the same persona that is Plath's plaster cast exterior she resents so much. I realised that this was always the objective of my question bowl, a kind of psychological undressing.

In attempting to undress psychologically, be intimate whether verbally or in the form of a text (zines being an example), the issue I always seem to hit against is permission. Where do I get permission to speak from?

My silly question bowl is definitely built upon the idea of permission. As soon as you play by its rules you *have* to speak and you *have* to listen. As well as being probing, it's an enforced kind of turn-taking. It eliminates competition, dominance, loud voices. Maybe that's also why I like it.

Self-help books will say this permission comes from 'within', that it comes from a sense of entitlement, and that we have to (re)learn to participate and trade intimacies.

While that's useful it doesn't ask why that permission was taken away, who took it away. Why are all these women silent? Why don't we feel entitled to take up space, to exist? And from there to ask, how do I want to speak, what do I want to talk about, what is my language like? And if I can't say it out loud, then I'll write it down instead, because I want to exist.

As a compulsive diary writer in my teens I turned practically mute at school, but wrote for hours at home. The less I spoke the more I wrote. I think I only felt safe dropping my guard in private.

Writing is a way of speaking when you are silent, and it aims for human connection even though as an act it's essentially solitary. A blank page is its own permission slip, it wants to be filled and anything you put upon it is immediately valuable because it's no longer contained but *out there* in the world. It can also be entirely on your own terms; you can be your only audience, you can be messy, imperfect, and experimental, it's up to you how you fill the space, and it's up to you if anyone chooses to see it. But I hope people *do* see it.

"Time and again I, too, have felt so full of luminous torrents that I could burst [...] And I, too, said nothing, showed nothing; I didn't open my mouth, I didn't repaint my side of the world" – Helene Cixous

July

Winded. The air is dead too. Gasping for a sparkly, sexy feeling that doesn't actually exist in real life unless you are fucking wasted. Or the night I took ex, or they called it molly (which I never knew how to spell), I took it in a port-a-potty, letting the chemical granules melt underneath my tongue. It always happened so that I ran into C., whose name has haunted me from the day my dad died. My new stepdad C.; my German Shepard C.; my newly dead father's middle name C.; and now my ex boyfriend, my first love C.

And there he is, my first lover; C., that last C. And we were sitting next to each other as we came up for the first time. Staring at the water, I wish I knew what body of water that was on the edge of Detroit, but I was learning different things:
how it was fun to barely be able to breathe. How A. loved it so much she'd go back every year. I only ever got concerned about drugs after the second or third time taking it. Everyone always kept going without me except with alcohol.

July

I was twenty, he said he liked that I was 20 a lot when we first met. Maybe that's where him and his ex-lover left off. I never thought about that then. But this is before him, when I had heartburn for a couple months, a couple months that I happened to think I was heartbroken because of K. So I moved in with my sister, into her little apartment, and I fucked B. for no reason on the top bunk in the middle of the afternoon. I want to say that that sex was almost rape now, because I didn't want it at all, but for some reason that's always what turned me on about B. He was such an asshole that I never really wanted him; I just wanted him to want me.

September

Oh sweet September, how you ceaselessly remind me of that fake meaning that I always want to find. The paper coffee cup, the books I'm studying, I'm sitting at a café picturesque always all of September picturesque. Where I meet M., at the café of course, but he is not right for my picture, oh no no no. But I am able to convince myself that he is perfect because he is hard to have. This is when I am the most alone in a good way, but I also smoke weed every night with E. who normally does more interesting things with her high like smash pumpkins or break tv sets. I just lay around dreaming up futures for other people who are less like me, so I don't do that much anymore.

In February, we drove up north to your stepdad's hunting cabin. The night before you asked the crowd at the show in your friend's one-room apartment where we'd be if we could go anywhere right then.

I said Chapel Rock; I forget why. So you said you'd take me and I pushed you down on my bed and kissed you and then we fell asleep. And the next day you really did take me but we didn't make it all the way. I remember how you offered me wine when I walked into your house. How I felt like I was cheating on M., how you wanted me to leave—eating cereal in your kitchen after—but I didn't, because that's the kind of girl I am.

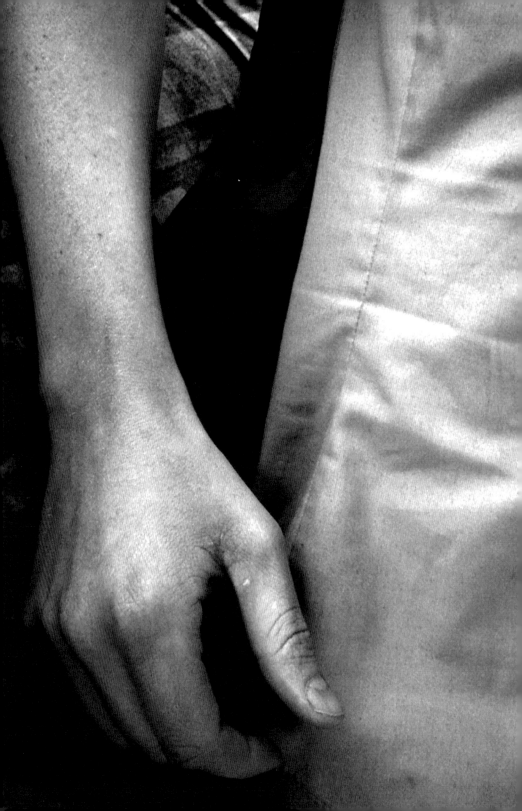

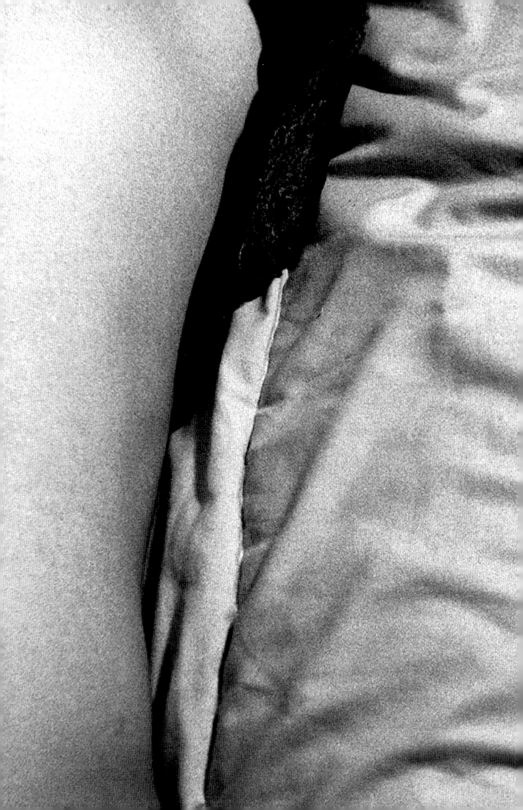

MILKY BLUE

I called a friend and we talked about the variables in crossing a street, like what if halfway across you realize that there is nothing on that sidewalk in front of you that will make you feel any different than you do here on this asphalt in the in-between and you just really can't be bothered to carry this mass of meat all the way to the other side because it seems to be getting heavier and the curb keeps rising and as much as you hate to be an inconvenience for the people in these cars you just need to sit down right

now.

A stranger once grabbed my body because I was presenting it to him by leaving my house, as though the sidewalk is a lawless lost and found. I was pulled into a friend's car by my hair where she quietly closed the door so that she could scream without bothering anyone. No sympathy for the sad.

Throw away cares and pretend that the couch is the dream. It's under the cushions, it's between the tiles on the floor. It's the sound of easy snoring while you have to will yourself into existence every morning. Sit to avoid white marble stairs coming up to meet your face.

Sit but then you're sitting at a swimming pool by yourself and your legs are swinging over the side, feet in water knees under palms. Swinging your feet just like you watched someone swinging theirs from the side of an overpass. There is no sympathy for the sad and I've never really helped anyone. Them in the dark and you in the water, always assuming that after they swung their legs over they swung them right back because there is solace to be found in using a rib cage as a pillow, and in letting someone buy you breakfast. I let

118

someone buy me breakfast, and over pancakes I ground my teeth down to smaller and smaller waves. Pool bottom elbow scabs don't keep me floating. From hot to warm to empty cup, I put tea bags against my eyes in the hopes that I could see the future in the leaves. I saw vomit in a bonfire and my own feet trailing up some stairs, which is the closest I'll ever get to flying. These aren't dreams but things I remember through telling, experienced through repetition. As clearly as though I ate it for breakfast. I spoke them through the tiny hairs on my tongue shed from body parts that you've never cared with, only used for a sense of purpose because without giving me mine you wouldn't have one.

A person made of raked up leaves, I knew it was just dust mites moving under your skin simulating a hug and a hand hold. You told me to fuck off as if I was there for you, and then you fell asleep holding my hand like it can be so nice to do. The knees of my jeans were all stretched out along with my fingers reaching for bottles of whiskey that weren't mine. Nothing was mine except for the head ache.

You're living the love life of a magician. Rub your lover's back until they bend like a spoon, cut off their legs until they fall in Stockholm syndrome with you. You have bad luck so they have to learn how to turn us into fools. Sucker punch until slack jaw, sweet talk until sick.

I'm not sure what kind of person I was before spitting bits of you back at you, but now I exist to mingle with the fish bones stuck in the back of your throat. I swear I was drinking water.

In the last year
i have only loved the kinds of men with darkness
in their minds and bad habits
the ones who can't cope with the demands of
masculinity
but would never articulate that that
way, because masculinity has already fermented
at the output of nuanced verbal admissions or omissions
ones whose intensities i recognize to the exclusion of
cultural, educational, or class markers
with whom i am in no way intellectually compatible,
nor even stylistically,
but "i like your intensity" in the deleuzian way—
where force, fierceness, desperation extract a response

> there is much to love about the word desperate
> its origins are hopeless, without a hope,
> which is to say without one hope, a single hope;
> the kind of hopeless which is actually just hope in everything

as if i see them all nude. i will them nude
to travel them across time, economic status, and geographical location
i have been experimenting with my love for a long time

i have been hanging out in the gutter
exploring what boundarylessness can afford me
for most of my life,
a parallel truth with less distance:
i have only loved impossible women
women who are taken but love me, too
who tell me with their nerves
by patrolling their own militant disaffection
or by lingering too long
over a sheer shirt when i'm not looking

straight girls who confess and lean but never pass the brink
or the ones whose strength of character matches my own
we intimidate each other away
like south-south poles of magnets
you are afraid of women and you should be
these are the women who are masochists
they elicit fear with their magnanimity
so they like men who disregard them
to transcend woman's formidability is a supernatural feat
if phallic power is anything, it is assumption
that particular quality of oblivion which can dismiss even the extraordinary
without knowing

SOFIA YURIKO BACA

DESTROY YOUR BODY

I've dated punks, I've dated punk rockers, squatters, crusties and dread-heads. They all stank. Every one of them. They stank like the end of music festivals. The smell of sewered-on fields, beer, whiskey, the sour smell of weed, lighter fluid, spunk-filled latex condoms, piss, sick. The sick smell was more like the after-sick. The aura of the post-vomit, the gastric acids on the breath via the burnt oesophagus, acid eroding the tooth enamel, convulsing tongues licking at dried mouths.

They all vomited in front of me at one stage or another. Some in strategic moves to purge their stomach to make way for another alcoholic watering. Some just before sex to straighten out, and some in the morning but then I'd

usually be at it too by then. Ha ha! At first I thought it was gross but then I grew to really love the vibe of someone who had just thrown up. I dunno, there's something really visceral, really real about a guy who's just puked and in the next moment is picking up his axe and getting back to work.

Every one of them had waxy clothes, stiffened by spilt bong juice, mud, sweated on, slept in, even their fingers were waxy. If they touched my face or body, it felt like I was being caressed by a Barbour jacket. I bet if they'd have rubbed their fingers together they would eventually rub the layers of sediment on their skin into little tiny black dirt balls. Even their boogers were black. They showed me on occasion. They would take their silt entombed, overgrown fingernails and shove them up their dirt freckled noses, root around mining for the clumpy, sticky paste.

Before we would have sex I would force each and every one of them to shower with soap. I would get them all revved up, we'd get to a serious dry-hump stage, then I would say, you know, "dude, you gotta get clean". Then I would go to

123

the bathroom, switch on the shower and hand them a bottle of shower gel. Their hair would always stink but it's the body that counts in that circumstance. I can boil wash my cheap pillows. I can't boil wash my insides.

The reason I'm telling you this, the reason I want you to know is because, well I'm no phony imposter ok? I created myself too.

I remember the first time I saw you, GG. You were pacing out the back of the Poolbar in downtown LA before your show. You looked so fucking hot. I knew then, right then, in an instant that I wanted you. Some people called you a neanderthal, a shitbag, a buddy of mine once told me that your old high school teacher described you as a wolverine. I liked that! The next day I looked up the definition of a wolverine: the Wolverine is a stocky and muscular carnivore, more closely resembling a bear. It has short legs, a broad and rounded head, small eyes and short rounded ears and is the size of a medium dog.The Wolverine has a reputation for ferocity and strength out of proportion to its size, it has the ability to kill prey many times larger than itself. Like many other mustelids, it has potent anal scent glands used for marking territory and sexual signalling.

I thought that was particularly apt for you. You, the underground messiah, the human animal - Public Animal No.1. Your body is a rock n roll temple. Your flesh, blood and body fluids are a communion to us. You are Jesus Christ, God and the Devil. You created Elvis. You, the commanding leader and terrorist of rock 'n' roll. Even before you were born you were plotting. You are the one throwing all the monkey wrenches into the gears. Nobody has your endurance, baby. Nobody has the endurance to finish what they were set out to fucking do!

Oh GG, I ache for you. I woke up so sad this morning. I dreamt that you were dreaming about me. In my dream I wake up and discover that you'd left a voicemail on my Dad's house phone during the night. So when I woke up this morning I checked and there was no message. I keep recalling the message you leave in the dream.

That time by the dumpsters, before

124

the show, I swear you noticed me. Did you see me? I looked over, I could make myself out in the refection of your mirrored aviators. Did you feel the connection? I swear you blushed, was it colour in your cheeks or dried blood? I carry that moment with me everywhere now. I know you don't believe in compassion but I imagine you vulnerable, needing me. I imagine you the moment after you slammed that microphone into your mouth and knocked out all your teeth. The pain you must have been in, the comfort you must have needed.

I gotta say, I love the way your mouth looks now. Your Fu Manchu mustache really frames it. It's handsome. I like the way your upper lip is loose, you look older. I guess your skin drapes over your facial structure, which makes it way more expressive. Do you even eat now? Or do you eat through a straw? My Grandpa lost all his teeth and now he gurns a lot. His whole jaw bone is dissolving away, my Dad was telling me that the chewing pressure stimulates the bone. He told me that eventually the bone will shrink and the nerves will become exposed. I wonder what it must be like to chew gum with no teeth?

Someone once referred to you, *an angry Dad* once referred to you as the devil himself rendering you a nightmare, he said "you.. are.. a.. nightmare! You're a nightmare!". I watched that footage from the Springer show. It was hilarious.

Those stupid assholes will never understand you.

Poem For Nesting

Boys are ruiners, you said-
but not this boy. Often I would look
at your shortcut hair, our matching
pallid colours; squawks, to try and bring out
in me what I thought was missing.
Here, the river, and here the sea, and always canals
and annals of watery trash that follow my
trudging heels.
You were not there in those endless car-rides
and lifeless landscapes. I remember roads
more than anything. But now, remembering
our hours i feel a heavy stack on my throat.
My words are clinging: clambering into the
stale conditioned air. But they were always
carried like a hoarse whisper, a hearse
for kinship, and I was always a mewling cat in a box.
Oh well.
A friendship is like a collage and
oh damn, I walk my trail of slime
to the supermarket and back, to a desk, to
a bar, to a house. Each way I lose a
silvery minute of our history. I slip on newspaper
nests all neatly ripped to mimic a photographic
visage. It is always left out in the rain. I pool
together every you I have collected.

ALANNA McARDLE

of attraction

girls twirl fucks through their fingers
wishing for knots to pray on, pulling hard
at the thread, first to make a motion
towards unraveling, then naked.
drink, what else is there to do? scream.
i've heard that before, from upstairs,
a room i only remember being in last
year at a party: togas, they made me
kneel, drink from a turkey baster full
with rumor, and wine, and some
other purple burn. tonight is cold, i sleep
with my mouth wide open.
in the bathroom down the hall
with the broken fan whirring
someone is fucking in the shower.
it doesn't matter who, some wild
cowboy probably. what if john wayne
was actually just another asshole
with pretty blue eyes and what if i
was one too? then i'd vomit all over,
i'm really not kidding, i'd vom with purpose.
this house makes sound when it is empty
and i blame the ghost.
she was pretty too, once, until
she killed herself (they say),
game over. i'd like to walk
into the woods and make a mess
of leaves, in my hair and boots,
and i want to smell like cloves
in unmoving air, and i want to be
hopped up on how it feels to plunge
a finger into moss, like long dreams.

KATIE FOSTER

1. "don't say that just yet. we don'twant it to be that."

2. a grandson approaches his grandfather at a funeral. at their goodbye the older man says, "you call me grandpop. why is that?"

3. the old man's brother played violin in the big city's symphony. he was a machinist at merck and first his hands were wrecked and then his stomach became a bag and after the cancer took his mind the machinist couldn't help my mom with her high school math homework anymore.

4. the big city is williamsport forty miles west. did you know the high school football team up there is called the millionaires? did you?

5. connellsville has a carnegie library and a downtown with a riteaid and blight and once it had the highest number of millionaires in the united states and i guess the world. once carnegie had the pinkertons set a river of coalcrackers on fire, bloody homestead strike, 1892.

6. shamokin's a town you could buy for a dime

7. "these are the people welfare was invented for, emma. they were POOR before it hit. i mean poor."

8. but up here barns are still left to fall, and tarpaper is still seen. a conagra truck rides a truckbuckled highway past sawed off mountaintops. a teenager stands at the edge of a field with a pacifier in his mouth staring and sucking he is standing there just staring and sucking

9. my grandfather was a machinist and my grandmother stayed home. home is in the hills and during the air raid cold war shake rattle and roll sixties a highway rocked through them. depth charge rock falls and sometimes the kids didn't make it to school sometimes they hid in the coal bin beneath the porch to miss it. one of my aunts is a lunchlady and the other's a line cook. one of my uncles cans pasta at the conagra plant and one is a garbageman. one of my uncles sits on his front lawn all day spitting shaking and turning

128

yellow. I-80's path of destruction

10. my mom's freshman year at college her tv got stolen and some older boys picked the lock on her door.

12. "he would've gotten a real kick out of you guys. he would of said that you're perfect."

13. no, he didn't see my mom graduate. if you'd deny luck, do you have it on your side?

14.

BIG MONEY

i play a loud show in a run-down beach town. even inside the damp stucco
bar i can smell the ocean. there is no stage. i stand in front of a small square
window with crusted glass, bright snatches of palm filling the frame.
after the show the band lingers on the sidewalk, swapping cigarettes with the
bartender, hours on end. my eyes ringed red. mathew yawns. he trails the
hem of my shorts with his finger. i could stay up all night, i say. he smiles,
leaves for the apartment with the amps and the guitars and my wet kisses all
over him. i sit legs-crossed in tamara's two tone civic. in her cd player: led
zeppelin. i try not to notice. it is easy to forget: windows open, hair sticking to
the sides of my lips.
down the 710, across the bridge to san pedro, past massive red and purple
crates, blue cranes piercing the orange-black sky. we park on west paseo del
mar, and hop the fence, and clutch each other's hands as we slip down a
muddy bank littered with slabs of concrete crawling with graffiti. we perch on
a rusted pipe and watch the sun rise. we drink cold coffee cut with crème de
menthe. the mint makes my mouth tingle, warms every part of my body. the
sunrise is muted. nothing but pink tinged fog. we watch anyway.
when she drops me outside my apartment, she says i'll call you tomorrow
about venice. i am too tired to wonder if she will.
i unlock the door, cat keening on the stoop. the roommates are not awake. i
open all the windows and let the clean white sunlight fall in neat lines all over
my floor. i lay down on the hardwood, sun hot on my thighs. i read pamela
des barres' memoir i'm with the band, a juicy afternoon treat. i fall asleep on
the floor thinking of jimmy page with a suitcase full of whips, mick jagger
giving head two hours straight, lips swollen. i sleep hard.

4.15.15
Long Beach, CA

¯_(ツ)_/¯

shruggal chat
09/03/2015

Grace:
Babs! After thinking about it non-stop all last week I forgot that tonight is when we were gna do a discussion all together for the chapess
It would only need to be 15-20 mins I reckon
If anyone is around later just msg and I'll hop on or we could leave it til another time
Camille:
oh yeah!
i am just on fb at work doing nothing
so if you wanted to do it sooner that'd be fine
in fact it'd be better
my phone died
so either between now and 9pm
or at like 10pm
Grace:
Ooooh cool. either works for me. Let's see if anyone else is around soon!
I guess we could talk about international women's day?? I was offline pretty much all weekend so I've missed the memes

Camille:
idk if there are any memes
but i accidentally had a bender this weekend so i haven't rly looked at the internet
Grace:
Weeyyyyyyy
STAG
Camille:
haaaahh
Grace:
The only woman I saw on international women's day made me a sandwich in a cafe
Camille:
i spent it hanging out with owen and max and all their man friends and then at work
i saw some women for a bit
but not enough and not my faves
Grace:
Every day is that day to us so it's ok
Camille:
tru
Rosa:
You saw me Camille! Briefly
Available for chat whenever btw
Camille:
oh yeah!
can we talk about something more interesting
Grace:
Yeah of course
Camille:

132

idk what

maybs the grossest thing we've

ever done

Rosa:

Yes I second Camille

Omg that's a good idea but I can't

think of mine

Camille:

yeah me neither

it's a good concept tho

Grace:

Ahhhhh! Amazing

Mine would mostly be poo related

tbh

Camille:

everyone loves poo stories i

reckon

Camille:

this is unrelated

but i really feel like if the years and

years song can be a number one

then i can write a number one

not that the song is bad

it's abanger

but it's just like an unexpected

number one

Grace:

Oh I haven't heard it

You could def write a number one

song!!

Camille:

it's a really good song

Grace:

Omg them!!

I met the singer

So dreamt

*dreamy

Camille:

when?????

Grace:

A few years ago, one of my ex's

friends is their friend

Camille:

I KNEW I WOULD KNOW

SOMEONE WHO HAS MET

THEM

Grace:

Haven't seen them play

Plus like, it was literally a few mins.

I doubt they'd remember me.

Camille:

doesn't matter I just knew id know

someone who had met him and I

was right

Grace:

You're magic

Camille:

I just made the best ever pasta

sauce

Grace:

I just had some life changing tofu

Camille:

what a day

what was the tofu like why was it

life changing?!!

Grace:

It was fried to perfection

What about you??

Camille:

m8

so like
ingredients: onion, garlic, leek,
spinach, pure, flour (for thickening)
almond milk, cheese, tvp,
nutritional yeast
Grace:
Oh my goddddd
That sounds so gorg
Camille:
can't even believe something so
beautiful could be made by me
Grace:
Everything you make is beautiful
Rosa:
i second that
Camille:
waaaaah
Grace:
ok so one of the grossest things
I've done (that I can remember) is
When me and my best friend at
school stayed out in my nanna's
tiny tiny camper van. Like we
insisted on doing it rather than stay
in my room. Or maybe my Nanna
had to stay in my bed idk. But we
were having such a great time, and
then suddenly we started thinking
about scary things, and became
convinced jack the ripper was
underneath the van.
After that we were too frightened to
move rly. But I suddenly needed a
poo. We tried opening the door and
seeing if we could get out but we

just imagined his arm sweeping out
and pulling us under.
So the only option was to poo on a
piece of kitchen roll. Which I did,
natch. Oh my god guys you cannot
imagine the intolerable smell. My
friend was fixated on it, like couldn't
look away as it was happening.
And then before we both vommed I
balled up the kitchen roll and threw
it out the window. And I think it
splatted on my mum's best friend's
car
Why have I just told this story
Camille:
oh my god that's amazing
that is truly incredible
Rosa:
Oh
My
God
Ruth:
Haha... one day you need to meet
my friend Sam, she has a wealth of
poo-related stories
Rosa:
Grace you are my hero my total
hero
Grace:
shades emoji
Ruth:
All her favourite stories have poo
in.
Camille:
does anyone else have one?

Grace:

Rly early on in our relationship me n Andy were trying to ask each other unexpected questions and for some reason I asked 'how many times have you pooed not in a toilet?' and he was like WHAT lolllll

Rosa:

One of my earliest memories, and certainly the earliest of my memories in which my rebellious streak came out

Grace:

Pls guys, you can't leave me alone out here with that story

Rosa:

I was toilet trained like I totally knew where poo should be

But I remember, really clearly, standing in my living room and realising I needed a poo

But I didn't want to go to the toilet

So I just did it in my shorts and then shook it out onto the carpet

Do wot I want

Grace:

Rosa *heart eyes emoji*

Ruth:

One time, I remember watching the cat poo on the carpet. And my mum had to clean it up.

Then I remember needing a poo and just did it wear the cat did.

Grace:

OMFG incredible

Camille:

this is all so amazing

Grace:

"That must be where poo goes"

Do you have one Camille?

Ruth:

I think I wanted to wind my mum up actually. I knew it was wrong.

Camille:

I have a sad one and a poo one

Rosa:

RUTH OMG amazing

Can we all just poo in the wrong place plz

It could be like our gang tag

Camille:

yeppp

Rosa:

"There's been a shruggal about"

Camille:

hahahahahahahaha omfg

Grace:

Haaaaaa

Oh my god

Yeah I think if we said the ages we were in those stories it would make it funnier

Ruth:

My story was from yesterday

Grace:

Ruth marry me

Rosa:

Ruth *hearts*

Camille share yours! Sorry I got too

excited about wild pooing

Camille:

sad or poo?

Grace:

WILD POOING

Both, unless sad one makes you sad

Rosa:

And always your choice

Camille:

i'll do sad then poo, my poo one is kinda similar to grace's

sad one: it was when i was very ill with an eating disorder and i was binging/purging a heck of a lot but i was scared of my parents hearing because they'd listen out for the toilet flushing lots so one day i started vomming into like empty containers and just put them under my bed and they all just stayed there for months but then i sorta forgot about them and yeah it was terrible

sorry that's a horrible thing

Grace:

Ohhhh cammile

xxxxx

Ruth:

 That must have been miserable :(:(

Camille:

so poo one: i was at a house party and i needed a poo but the toilet was very blocked so i pooped into

a bunch of toilet paper and replaced the can of beer in the plastic bad i had with the poo and walked through the party out into the street and put it in a bin

but like walked through the party with the poo in a bag

holding a beer

Grace:

You. Are. The actual queen.

Ruth:

Problem solved.

Camille:

i guess it was the most polite thing to do ?

Grace:

v polite

Camille:

also thank you for being nice about the sad one xxxxxx you guys ruuuule eating disorders drooooool and pooping also rules

Grace:

Pooping and eating rule, Camille rules, I'm so sorry that happened to you but I can completely understand it and I don't think it's gross rly. Not to minimise it at all. But it seems like a v natural reaction to hide it like that.

ily bb

Camille:

yes definitely and like all normal logic was totally gone at that time *hearts*

Rosa:

I can't stop thinking about poos I've done now

Which is nice

Grace:

Tell us more poos!! I am still so pleased with the idea of you shaking it out of yr shorts.

Rosa:

I think one poo I did is the reason I'll never go to end of the road festival

Camille:

hahhh what a sentence

Rosa:

It was the last morning and I went to a dreaded portaloo to do a poo

Long queue and I knew the portaloo would be horrific

And I got there and did it and you know how portaloos have that flap? Yeah it just lay there, right across it. Evenly layed out so the flap didn't flap

So I tried flushing it vigorously

Grace:

Oh noooo

Rosa:

But you know how portaloos do that flushing with its own contents instead of blue liquid when they're not cleaned out regularly enough

Camille:

ohhh nooooooo

Rosa:

Yeah I was trapped in a hot plastic smelly box with a fountain of beery piss trying desperately to wave my poo goodbye

Grace:

Oh godddd

Rosa:

And I was just there pulling and balking and pulling and balking

I can't even remember if I got rid of it in the end, I was probably defeated tbh

Grace:

Oh fuck, so grim

Rosa:

I should probs say that apparently the toilets there have got better since that year

But I don't care I just can't do it again

Camille:

that's too much for anyone

Ruth:

I would have just left it and ran out screaming. Make the most of it.

Grace:

That thing of desperately trying to get rid of a poo is def bringing up some haunting memories

I bet the others have some good stories

Ruth:

You know how cats desperately try and cover their's up and fail miserably? That's like humans but with poorly flushing toilets.

Rosa:

I don't want anyone to ever see my poo unless I'm doing it into a kitchen towel in order to throw it out of a caravan window so that jack the ripper doesn't get me

Camille:

hahahahaha

Rosa:

And in that scenario I'd want *everyone* to see it

Grace:

shades emoji

Rosa:

Omg I've remembered a poo at a party

Where they didn't have toilet paper

So I found those little eye pads people wipe make up off with

But I was v close to using a towel because fuck anyone throwing a party without plenty of toilet paper

Camille:

TOWEL

Grace:

Haaaaaaaa oh god I've been in so many scenarios like that

Absolute torture

Ruth:

Is that the strangest thing any of us have wiped our bum with?

Rosa:

Apparently some people rip up the cardboard tube and use that?? Not

for me altho v ingenious congrats

Grace:

Oh there was the donut thing kitty said! Altho that was a friend

Eww yeah that sounds painful to me

Camille:

i've done the toilet roll thing

omg yes the donut thing

the toilet roll thing didn't work well

i was desperate tho

OH FUCK

Grace:

I'm trying to think..... I may have used newspaper when pushed???

Camille:

MEMORY

used a sanitary towel

Rosa:

But that was wiping piss and for some reason in my head that's worse than poo re donuts

Grace:

OH GOD. I ONCE USED A LEAF.

Wooaaahhhh it's all kicking off

Rosa:

I once used a posh tissue infused with Vicks vapour rub out of desperation

Ruth:

I had to use my own hand once.

Rosa:

Weirdly tingly in a discomforting but also "I've got a fun secret" kind of way

138

Grace:
This is so beautiful guys
Rosa:
Omg Ruth you are superior how did you even manage
Grace:
Right, weirdly one just happened to me right now.
Camille:
TELL
Ruth:
Seconded
Grace:
All this talk of poos must've 'fired up the kiln' (as andy says) so I went to the loo and mid-poo the kettle started whistling (cos I have a super old kettle and I forgot I put it on). So the second half of the poo was strangely stressful and difficult.
Like I couldn't just break off
Oh boy
What a boundary we have broken down guys
Camille:
the floodgates are open
the poo stories will never stop
Grace:
I love this
Rosa:
I went on a date with a guy once and he talked about poo too much
Like I obv love talking about it
But with friends ykno? I think first

date is a line
Unless your first date is making composting toilets or smth
Anyway he mentioned it at least twice, but the only one I fully remember is him looking at his beer and seeing it was quite sedimenty and then him saying he'd be on the toilet all night
Ruth:
"how can I make this date less awkward" "break the ice by talking about poo"
Grace:
Woooooah
Rosa:
Anyway I still kissed him because he was (at least visually) attractive and kissing is nice
Grace:
Yeah that's not something you want to imagine a relative stranger doing before you've even worked out if they're attractive to you
Rosa:
And then he texted me next day for a second date
Grace:
And it's Reuben??
Camille:
did u say "aren't you tired from being on the toilet all night?"
hah omg is it reuben?
Rosa:
So I replied telling him that I would

139

not and then gave him the constructive feedback of how he talked about poo too much

Grace:
Haaaaa

Camille:
amazing

Ruth:
OMG

Grace:
You are MY hero

Ruth:
That is the best thing anyone's done to turn down a second date. That is how dating should be done.

Rosa:
Haa no although Reuben didn't take much longer. I think it was maybe after second date he emailed to tell me he'd just had a power cut and was glad it didn't last longer than half an hour as he didn't wish to poo by candlelight. Dreamboat.

Camille:
amazing
the perfect amount of time to wait for the poo chat

Rosa:
My fav thing is to go for a poo at work during shift. Hold it on on break, do it while they're paying you

Camille:
yeppp!
had a surprise poo during work today
like didn't know it was gonna happen
pleasantly surprised
thank u bowels

Rosa:
My likes include TV, biscuits, cycling and doing all my poos at work

Ruth:
this is what people who don't sit down to wee miss out on

Rosa:
I love a sit down I really do
I don't get why boys don't sit down whenever they get a chance to, like at home or whatever. It's so nice!

Grace:
I love this so much!

Rosa:
Are you sat on a toilet right now grace

Grace:
I've always been a bit confused whenever anyone says they can only poo on their own toilet
Haaaaa

Rosa:
They are lying I am sure

Ruth:
yeah... I always feel smug after I've gone at work

Rosa:

I have no control if I need a poo I am going to have one

I mean I have control enough to hold it in until I find a toilet

Grace:

Yeah same!! I can't imagine holding it in for hours. Awful.

Rosa:

Gone are the days of shaking it out of my shorts

Camille:

hahhh

Grace:

I feel like I'd go green if I tried to hold it

Pls shake it out of your shorts one day, for us

Rosa:

When I've had to hold it in for a bit, it hurts and it also feels like it's definitely going to fall out

Maybe that's what Tay Tay's song is all about

Ruth:

HAHA

Rosa:

Probs not tho I've never told t swift my poo story

Camille:

hahahaha

what should my 10000th tweet be

Rosa:

The poo emoji

Kitty:

This whole thing is glorious

Camille:

YES

Kitty:

I love pooing and I love all of you

Idk if I have ant good poo stories but I just poo a lot

We have a weird pooer at my work

I think a lot of workplaces have one?

It's not me tho

Grace:

I think we all are that one

Ruth:

tell the story!

Kitty:

Someone pooed in the locker room and but apparently it was like... Presented on a bit of loo roll on the floor?

And about once a year someone manages to poo on the floor in the toilet off the corridor which is just like a disabled one not a cubicle

But I always feel like even if you somehow pooed on the floor by mistake you'd try and hide it??

Ruth:

They obviously get some kind of weird pleasure out of it.

Grace:

Oh dear lord

Ruth:

Or are drunk students?

Camille:

woahh
Grace:
Yeah that's def on purpose
Kitty:
I never understood how it could
even happen but actually one time
I had an IBS flare-up that was
really bad and did a tiny poo that
went on the floor (idek how I was
like doubled over in pain as I got
off the loo) and then I cleaned it up
ans washed the floor so
That is my personal poo on the
floor story but I was in my twenties
Grace:
Yeah I don't rly understand ppl not
cleaning up after themselves
Kitty:
But I think the phantom pooer must
get some enjoyment out of it
Grace:
Yeah that seems the only
explanation
Camille:
"phantom pooper"
*pooer
Grace:
"Presented on a bit of loo roll"
Camille:
sorry i just love the word poop
Kitty:
Also one time someone tucked a
used sanitary towel behind some
of the panelling in one of the loos
Grace:

Oh goddddd
Seriously not ok
Camille:
sad face
Rosa:
A girl at my school who was
supposed to be the sexy popular
one, like Regina George or cher
(Horowitz?) From clueless
Kitty:
And a man who used to work with
us found it cos it was peeking out
Ruth:
When I was a student we lived in a
massive student house and one
sunday I came down and someone
had pooed on a dining chair.
Rosa:
She once wrote a message on the
PE block toilet windows in her own
shit
Kitty:
Sunday funday
Omg amazing
What did it say?
Ruth:
No one owned up to it and me and
my friends had to clean it up.
Grace:
Woah. Was it a cry for help?
To all stories...
Rosa:
I don't know I think it was a
threatening thing
She did it to show off and assert

her dominance

Which she did well I guess

Grace:

Wow

Intense

Kitty:

ASSert her dominance

Wheeeeey

Rosa:

Oh Ruth. Would you own up to pooing on a dining chair? I'd definitely try to blame someone else

Also good work kitty

Kitty:

Thank you

Grace:

This is all too gorgeous

Ruth:

No but I have since had dreams that it was me and it's confusing because I mix it up with the pooing where the cat did memory

Camille:

hahaha

Rosa:

I have to go to bed now but I'm really excited to catch up on this thread tomorrow

Ruth:

I have to remind myself it wasn't me.

Rosa:

Also Ruth omg

Camille:

i'm gonna go to bed too so that i don't tweet anything and save my 10000th

Grace:

Is everyone gna be ok with the poo discussion going in a zine?

Camille:

yep

Rosa:

Yes

Grace:

It's fine if any of you wana be taken out

Ruth:

Can you take out my surname? Just because of work.

Grace:

Oh yeah I'll only use first names for everyone

And just refer to us as the shruggals

Ruth:

Nice swapping poo stories everyone.

Camille:

good work everyone

Grace:

It's been lush

All the trains I have ever taken run like scars across this
country and others.
I took a train in Eastern Europe and watched the burning
pink sun
set over fields and fields of sunflowers
and I knew you were going to die.
The boys outside the station made kissing noises at me
and I swore at them even though they were children
and couldn't understand me anyway.

I took a train across the width of England
stinkingly hungover
and I knew that this would be the last time I would ever see
you.
I watched a child make an elaborate bracelet out of rubber
bands and I was made
dizzy by her tiny moving fingers.

I took a train on a flat grey day up to a village with wet
bracken turned to mush and a graveyard
where I had to stop myself puking on Sylvia Plath's
headstone
even though I was falling in love with the man next to me
because the plainness and silence of painful death had
looked straight at me. Death did not say anything to me
because it was nothing at all.

A rabbit sprints across a field in my imagination
and the flat table-top of a pond dotted with white birds
skids along the horizon. Even though it is raining
a fire is burning on the side of a hill
miles away.

NAOMI BAGULEY

I TAKE MY MEDS EVERY DAY BUT DON'T DO THINGS TO HELP MYSELF OR I DON'T THANK MYSELF FOR TRY-ING EVERYDAY

I WALKED AROUND THE SUPERMARKET HUNGOVER AND SPACED OUT, KIND OF BUMMED OUT I DON'T KNOW WHY. I BOUGHT APPLES + NOODLES FOR NO REASON, I DIDN'T REALLY EVEN WANT ANYTHING. MY MEMORY OF WALKING HOME FELT MADE UP, WE LEFT THE PARTY AT 7AM, IT WAS A WEIRD BLUE AND MISTY AND DEWEY... I'M DOING O.K. BUT I JUST WANT TO FEEL A LITTLE BETTER.

FRESH ✦ FRESH FRESH

I WANT TO BE A WOMAN WITH SNAKES WRAPPED AROUND HER HIPS..

every letter is a love letter every letter is a love let every letter is a love letter every letter is a love letter - every letter is a love letter every letter

LAST NIGHT I CRIED BECAUSE I ATE TOO MUCH INDIAN FOOD AND BLOCKED THE SINK. WHEN I WAS ASLEEP HE CLEANED IT OUT BECAUSE HE DIDN'T WANT ME TO BE SAD ABOUT IT - THAT WAS A TOKEN OF HIS LOVE - I KEEP IT

146 *HEATHER DUNLOP*

In Limbo

I am in limbo,

the dissonance is unbearable.

I contradict myself, I am a cadence that will never be resolved.

An incomplete being, neither here nor there.

Fundamentally unstable and strange and awkward.

I am a work in progress that may never be complete.

So many people think they know me but

they couldn't be further from the truth -

I am changing and growing and shifting all the time.

A reflection

When she opened the door she couldn't believe how good it felt to be free
after years in that dusty room- sure she was just taking the first steps
towards freedom but it felt great to have hope! When she looked at her
reflection in the window she saw herself for the first time. Intoxicated by how
clean and fresh the air was outside, that's when she could finally breathe.

Seasonal Affective Disorder

22nd February

21:36

When you were in the bath just now you had all these perfect thoughts but that's always how it is. You always come up with the best phrases or sentences when you haven't got the chance to write them down. Swimming, cycling, in the sauna. Monday nights highlighted by new episodes of programmes you like; Girls, though did Lena Dunham write girls you could relate to? Maybe only fleetingly. 29, in debt, tiny flat no pets, fucking basic bullshit job, real world life.

Fresh meat, a documentary about people in the Navy. A bath. Purposefully taking it slow. Made it through Monday. At the very least the sky was blue and the sun was out today. Need to spend more time looking at these things when you walk to and from the bus stop rather than refreshing social media repeatedly. Constant coasting until payday, cycle of money in, money out.

23rd February

08:36

The worst part is that as soon as you get into work those thoughts you had on the bus are gone. You cannot replace them now. Watching the reflection of the traffic overtaking in the opposite window. The bus turns right, past a pointless business park and down alongside the tram tracks and the bleak as fuck 'Nana Wendy's kitchen'. Here where there is no pen and paper is where proper thinking can be done. Just another of these places. Thinking of that stage in a relationship where the extension of life and living together has overridden the intensity of what brought you together. Beautiful moments, kissing after the side light is off, before you mentally check out for the day. Stroking his bum cheeks with the tips of your fingers as he runs the hot water and squirts washing up liquid into the sink. Him in his boxers the last sight of him before you leave the flat. Today was a different bus. Last night was a later night. The late bus is the one with the group of girls who won't shut up. The regular older girls throwing shade on a new girl's emo music. "Turn it down!" You left your headphones at home but they will get off in a few stops anyway.

17:32

And then walking home. The sky ombre pastel like a 90's ice lolly. The whole day is off, later again. Its sun going down time and the birds are out and you're so in your head but you're enjoying your new purple coat, £12 from a charity shop. And the scarf and hat combination. God it's sunny but it's so cold. And the light can't get you now the sun is so low down in the sky. Should have worn gloves but never mind walking along, walking home. You're a normal person, you're alive you're living. Just walking home like so many others of us.

22:01

The intensity and pressure to make. Everything. Rushed through. Let's not waste any time. There's a body of work to be made. It won't make itself. Every waking thought is worthy of noting down. The Sims 3 is getting boring now. You're waiting for the elders to die. It keeps pausing, jumping, crashing.

You have got better things to do but then you do them and honestly the work is technically complete but it doesn't look as great as the first ne that's maybe why doing copies or editions of the same thing over an over is never going to work because some of them won't be as good but maybe that is the entire point of the thing. But an evening making disappointing art is surely better than an evening waiting for The Sims 3 to reload, waiting for your elder Sims to die. For the ghost dog to leave the lot so you can bin the urn as it is making the computer crash too much to load too much to load.

24th February

08:41
Creepy strands of grass rigid with frost. Ground sinks as you step over the shortcut. Childhood bedroom in winter, teapot of tea. Warm there, different to mould filled drafty houses of your adult life.

26th February
19:22
Street lights, house lights, static punctuating the dark. Signal man sits in his box low lit. Hum of the microwave. Train is rolling and gurgling. That feeling you get when you think of the Northeast. Particularly Teesside, Middlesbrough, Hartlepool by the water. Deep down the track in the ridged path to somewhere you can only go once an hour. Something described as rather wet, rather meaning stinks of piss. Revisiting the past in the present. Seeing the same people over again each time a new time. Pressing down harder each time.

CONFIDENCE

REJECTION

LOVE

SORE

EXCITED

DISSAPOINT-MENT

GRIEF

"O" FACE

LET DOWN

Having a Truth

Sometimes I wonder what life could have been like if I didn't have issues with my mental health. The signs started showing at age 8 when I had my first referral to a doctor for what my parents described as weird scary behaviour. I was refusing to wash because there I was insistent there were cameras hidden in the bathroom and every night, I'd wait till everyone was asleep and go unplug everything (resetting the time on the video player) then begin the epic task of paperclipping my curtains together, pinning the sides to the wall and cellotaping the underside to the windowsill. For years I've had numerous family members, friends, healthcare professionals and counsellors try and slot me into a neat and tidy box, bringing forward whichever key traits at the time were convenient.

People love to diagnose you. People love to also discredit you if what you're saying doesn't fit into the TV show version of that illness they've just watched on channel 4. Situations with people playing devil's advocate after you plucked up the courage to overshare are pretty common. Also, *'everyone is a bit OCD though right?!'*

I spent most of my teens and early twenties trying to slot myself into any semblance of confirmed identity linked to a specific diagnosis, desperate to settle on just one area so I could properly study it and figure out how the hell I could tackle it *properly*. I could tick boxes under so many headings but none of the list seemed to be *me*.

I had a pretty shitty childhood and the scars show openly on my person soon within meeting me. I don't hide myself away from people anymore, in fact quite the opposite. I spent so many years trying to have people believe me or be accused of *crying wolf, playing the poor card* or being an attention seeker (despite being super mild, introverted and awkward) that the older I got, the more I wore this shit on my sleeve.

At first being open felt strangely more like I was an attention seeker. We're socialised to not talk about really horrible things, can't possible damper people's spirits. On the flip, it's perfectly acceptable to never say you're doing great and instead use phrases like *'aye not bad, I'll be rate or will be when it's Friday.'* We can be full of morose in some ways but once any real shit is dropped, the glances of awkwardness and defensiveness from others as if you just offended them by existing and having a truth is blinding. My way of navigating through life was to keep quiet and every so often test the waters with key friends who may have proven themselves to have clear levels of empathy and understanding as well as being reassuringly trustworthy. Sometimes it worked and I found myself in periods of openness that was eye-opening, comparing my life, my experience, my ways with others helped me understand myself more and highlight the areas that were troublesome or where I could actually see and measure my own strength and resilience. Because I was so introverted and went through some gnarly shit at a young age, I became pretty self-reflective and wise to the bs of the world and other human beings around me. I became a wise ass when I actually opened my mouth and learned to build a pretty solid screen of protection around me, separating me from the tough surroundings but also any chance of other people getting in and fucking with me. People being nice made me uneasy and my school friends thought it was hilarious when they hugged me because I went totally stiff. One day on a caravan weekend with my best friend, I came out wearing a vest top and shorts to the reactions of her whole family, shock across all their faces but trying to style it out because they know if they mentioned anything I'd run back in the door and never come out.

I always have been and always will be a weirdo.

I remember reading a quote in a self-help book after my first breakdown aged 17, *'what happened to me is wrong but there is nothing wrong with me.'* I wrote it in my diary and thought about it a lot. While I understand of course that what happened to me in my short life so far wasn't due to my own actions and I wasn't deserving of it in some way, I couldn't settle with *'but there is nothing wrong with me.'* There was something wrong with me. I just couldn't quantify it, what was circumstantial was the calibre of why so many people are dependent on alcohol and drugs on tv documentaries, a common reason why people commit crime and end up in prison or develop a self-destructive approach to life. Because of my circumstance I never felt like I received the right approach toward my mental health. Instead it'd take one look at my record and then came the sympathetic head tilt and softened voice.

Since my first major involvement with mental health practitioners following that breakdown, I fought to hide my truth, I knew that shit couldn't be cured, I knew there wasn't a pill or therapy to make that go away so I desperately pushed it away, out of the front of my brain as best I could to focus on the things my brain was doing on the daily that was making life hard for me. I walked out of sessions or became angry with counsellors who just wouldn't let my history go, they wanted to dredge everything up and focus on it entirely. It pissed me off no end.

When I was 21 I had my second breakdown. I never properly closed the chapter on the last but instead forged a life for myself in a new city with new friends and a more culturally aware existence, away from my working class roots and the extended family members who ridiculed me for having morals and chastising their inappropriate and offensive language. Unfortunately though, I was still running away from the things I didn't wanna talk about and also still struggling to find the right healthcare worker to work through my mental health struggles adequately by listening to me instead of making a judgement from my record before meeting me.

At 27, going into 28 I had my biggest breakdown to date and I realised I needed to sort my shit out. Prior to this I had been living for a number of years as a near full on recluse. I had been diagnosed as an agoraphobic with my OCD being worse than ever. The primary diagnosis Generalised Anxiety Disorder. I had slowly driven myself into a dark hole, turning against myself, reassuring myself this was simply a choice that made me feel better and that this was just *me*.

If this story sounds erratic it's because it was. I'm also telling it in the stages of how I looked at myself, my life and my health. It chopped and changed whenever I felt cornered to think about it. My obsessive brain would also constantly try and make sense of the unfathomable and when it's in your own head, it spins you right out.

Each breakdown came around the time of a trauma – the first after my grandad and significant caregiver died. The second when I was burgled. The third after going bankrupt, losing everything I had including the business I had set up with a view to finally cementing a positive future and then a few months later surviving a horrific attack.

It wasn't until that third struggle that I truly was able to stand still and reflect how my shit was out of control. There *was* something wrong with me and I needed to sort it out. It didn't matter if it was linked from a trauma, or if it was a chemical imbalance, it didn't matter if I was struggling to leave the house one day or manically destroy items from my past. I was *alive.*

I was one human being with one life to live and I was alive.

Seeing two therapists was one of the main open eye moments for me. It broke my life down into segments where you could only discuss that one area and that's when I realised – when a regular person has an issue or trauma, that is dealt with by a professional in that field. For me, I'd seen a *lot*. To an extent, as much as I never wanted to identify in this way – I was a frigging *case.* But you know what, I am *me.*

I don't need a diagnosis because it isn't as easy as that. I don't need to be linked to what happened to me every day because that's not my identity. I am a human being who wanted to be heard, I want to be happy, I want to be challenged, I want to be loved. These wants will inexplicably be linked to the losses and traumas in my life but they will *not* lead them. I will.

For the last year and a half I've been trying to live my most authentic life and get to a point when I can work towards being my best self. The progress in that time has been massive. I stopped trying to quantify and segment, instead I put everything into the pot, consulted specialist help and properly gave meds a go (something that always scared me before). I started sharing my story (every aspect of my life – good, bad, grey areas, honesty, denial, hope) and watched my progression through each diary entry. I connected with others who were struggling and surviving – talking real talk and having that much needed opportunity to get a little dark sometimes but also looking into how I can be a better citizen of the world, how I can be a better friend, how I can succeed and achieve my goals. Being open about my past but also sharing my *true* feelings no matter how vulnerable they make me feel, after years of hiding, denial, despair, struggle and confusion – I finally got real. It's been a tough time but I've shown I can survive this shit. It's still tough but I'm still sharing, still growing and understanding myself to better communicate every damn day.

I got this.
You got this.
We got this.

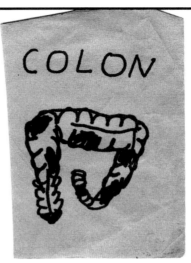

somewhere inside this fleeting home (this tired body), there is a garden.

the garden lives, softly pulsating, as a hidden swamp/stinking paradise.

in my garden, my grief roots and grows. my regret bends and rots. my loss lies on its side as a log, hosting the soft mounds of regret(s) that grow on its underbelly [in the damp lack of light].

in the center of my garden, a deep well reaches down into soil, further than even I could measure or know. my pain(s) loop(s) through like nitrogen - through the mud and into the leaves/ they drop as tiny fruits for my creatures to eat.

GARDEN

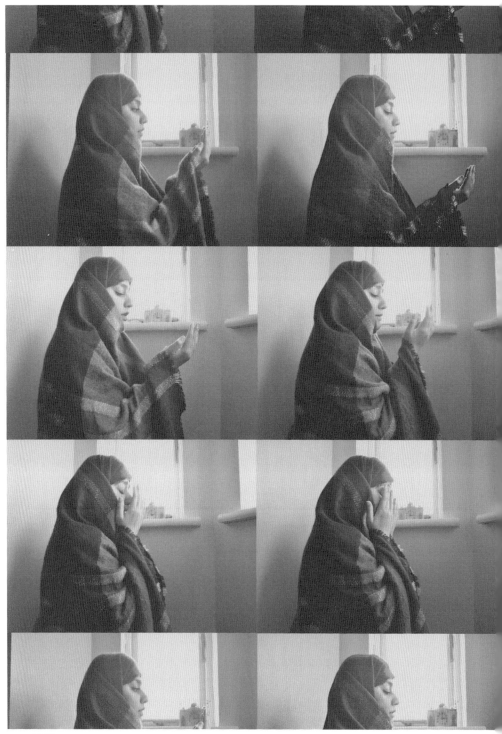

SAFFA KHAN

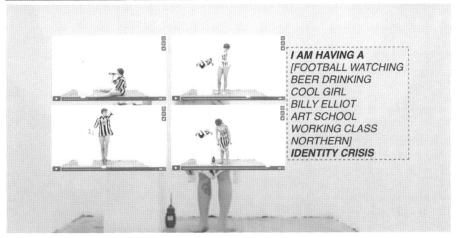

I AM HAVING A
[FOOTBALL WATCHING
BEER DRINKING
COOL GIRL
BILLY ELLIOT
ART SCHOOL
WORKING CLASS
NORTHERN]
IDENTITY CRISIS

GEORGIA GRACE GIBSON

159

RADI
ANCE
OV 1000
SUNS

A beginners guide to zine making

how + why to get involved now

The following text originally appeared as a free hand out put together by the team at Salford Zine Library. It's the direct result of the workshops we've led over the last 18 months and the feedback we've received. We know it can be helpful to have something to take away. Photocopy these pages, use this as a resource, add to it.

A zine (pronounced zeen as in magazine) is most commonly a hand made, photocopied, or otherwise cheaply produced small circulation, self published leaflet/comic/literally any other collection of printed paper you can imagine. Zines have historically been a way for groups and individuals to express opinions and ideas that may fall outside of the remit of traditional publishing and self publishing has offered us an alternative. In making a zine you are effectively your own editor, publisher, distributor and boss!

There are no particular skills or experience required, anyone with a pen and an idea can make a zine!

Zines can help us make a tangible connection to our own personal histories and in turn can help ground us in the present. Zine making can be a great way to engage with your community, make friends, share stories and document our experiences. Many zine makers sell or swap their zines through the mail, online, or at gigs, zine fests and libraries.

The DIY ethos at the heart of zine making promotes, and encourages the idea that everyone has the potential to be an artist/writer/musician/whatever you want. If you're not seeing/reading/hearing the media you want around you make it yourself!

Over the next few pages you'll find some tips and ideas for making your own zine. The thing with zines is there isn't really a right or wrong way of doing it, but it can help to have some pointers to start you off. Chances are you've picked this up at a zinefest or workshop, so you're halfway there already.

If you're not sure what you want to make a zine about you could make a collective zine, with contributions from different people on a certain topic, more on that over the page.

What's a comp zine?

A compilation zine, group zine or collective zine is a zine with contributions from more than one person. It can be a great way to bring together different opinions on a subject or celebrate our shared histories and experiences. It could be made in aid of an event, around a particular celebration or to bring together all sorts of things (community groups, student groups, fans (of anything) groups of friends, anyone at all – really ANYONE. It could just be for fun. A fanzine is a zine about anything you are a fan of.

OK, how do i get started?

Decide on your subject, this sounds obvious but be as specific as you can. Maybe you want to make a zine about an obscure tv show, the place you live, your favourite band (i.e. it can be literally anything) Are you looking for submissions from particular groups of people or with a certain slant, what kind of content do you want? (text, illustration, photos etc or perhaps a mix)

I recently put together the 2nd issue of Grub zine. The idea was simple; it would include recipes, my own and other peoples' as well as food stories, memories, writing. This sounded pretty vague even to me when i put out the call out for submissions so i decided to gather together some of the kind of writing i loved, that was the kind of thing i was looking for. I posted a flyer on my blog and twitter account (more on that in a bit) along with links to writing online which fitted the bill, this meant i could re-visit the list for inspiration, add to it, and share the vibe with people considering submitting.

Having twitter (or any social media presence i'm sure, but twitter works for me) helps. It's an easy way to let people outside of your immediate social cirlcle know about your project. It's no secret that the internet can be a great way of making friends, making zines kind of opens you up to a whole world of people that are into the stuff you're into/that you're making zines about. If you love it/care about it/want to share it i guarantee there will be other people getting excited about it too.

164

Useful info to put on the call for submissions:

A deadline, this can be whenever you want, it could be way off in the future but this will be an important factor for folks to consider if they want to apply.

If you're going to print the zine in black + white this could be helpful to know, particularly if people are sending you images. You might want to mention what size the zine's gonna be, if that seems relevant too.

You could put some prompts or ideas on the call for submission, or leave it totally open to interpretation. Here's an example of one from our pals at Ube zine

Ube contemporary art + writing

CALL FOR SUBMISSIONS

ON: DRESS TO ubezine@gmail.com

DEADLINE : 31st JULY 2016

So what do i do with the call for submissions? Will people really send me things?

Once you've got your little flyer/poster/however you want to think about it you can print them – give them to friends, leave them in places for people to find (library, college, wherever) and/or post it online, social media is great because people can easily share it etc. Attach it to emails, tweet your call out to @SalfordZineLib, we're happy to share it online.

Particularly if this is your first foray into zine making it can be a major worry that people won't send you anything, or they won't send you anything in time. You'll mention it to your mates and they'll all be really enthusiastic but actually not submit anything. Try not to worry about any of this stuff. If you don't get as many submissions as you want, extend the deadline, approach people directly (irl and online) whose stuff you'd love to include; what's the worst that could happen, they don't reply to your email?

Remember, if the zine you're making is kind of niche it might be hard to get those submissions rolling in, but it just means that when they do it'll be totally worth the wait. We're making this stuff because it doesn't already exist. Be patient; the reward of self publishing is in creating something that perhaps helps people to see things in a different way.

Things to consider:

Do you want your full name/real name attached to the zine? People use pseudonyms for all sorts of reasons, and sometimes zinesters do, particularly if their zines are very personal, or separate from their work/professional life. It's totally up to you + you will know if this point is relevant to you.

Whether you use your full name of not you might want to set up an email account for the zine (as much as anything this makes it easy to keep track of submissions) eg. For Grub zine i set up write2grub@gmail.com

You could start a blog/twitter/facebook page is that's your style. It can help to

166

have a hub to post updates on your project, particularly if you're thinking of doing more than one issue. But none of this is essential to zine making. I guess also remember you don't have to have all of this figured out just yet, first things first get making.

Practical tips

Once you've gathered everything you want to include you're ready to go. It might be a mixture of cut n stick, computer print outs and/or files on the computer.

There is no right or wrong way of putting together zines. You might want to cut, stick and write directly onto folded sheets of paper and then photocopy them. You might want to work on your layouts on Photoshop, Indesign, Publisher or something similar. I use a free program called Scribus (download it from www.scribus.net) which is pretty similar to InDesign and super easy to use. You might want to use a combination of both, and make each page by hand, scan them in and place them onto a template on the computer. If you're really stumped you could Google zine layout ideas. You could even check out YouTube for simple book-binding tutorials if you wanna get creative.

After years on making + photocopying my zines by hand i decided to digitise my process when i started putting out bigger print runs. I made maybe 25 copies max of lots of my early zines. Over the last few years the Chapess has been my main zine project. Each issue has print runs of around 100 and i re-print them regularly. Making the zines available as PDFs meant i could easily print multiple copies (i email the PDF to my printer and i pick them up as completed folded and stapled zines – chat to your printrer about this to see what services they offer/if the copiers can staple as they print...more tips for dealing with printers later) Having each issue available as a PDF also meant i could easily share it via email – this was particularly helpful with the Chapess as i could share it with contributors from around the world, saving us both some serious cash on postage.

Think about what's gonna work for you. Consider your print run/how many you can afford to print. How 'neat' do you want it to look anyway? Folding and stapling can actually be really good fun, especially if you get some mates round to lend a hand.

Printing

This is probably the least enjoyable part of making zines, but it doesn't have to be a chore. If you're copying your pages yourself get friendly with your local newsagents. Some of the bigger ones will have a photocopier you can use yourself for cheaps.

When I say it's a chore what i really mean is we all inevitably leave it til the last minute and end up either paying way above the odds in a professional printers or running around looking for somewhere to print them and/or arguing with old dudes in print shops.

I cannot stress enough building a rapport with your printer. You don't have to be best mates with them but if you can find somewhere that knows what you're after and is willing to either let you get on with it or print them exactly how you want them you're onto a good thing. Maybe you can scam copies at work or have a friend with a student card, either way make sure you give printing some thought.

Not everyone feels comfortable with a stranger copying their zines. If you want some one to one time with a copier scout out somewhere beforehand. Libraries are good but tend to be quite pricey. If you're a student use your student print shop, chat to them about exactly what you want, that's what they're there for. U-Print in the basement of Manchester uni SU on Oxford road is open to the public! Maybe other uni printshops are too i'm not sure, but it's worth finding out. U-Print are consistently helpful and reliable plus the price and print quality is A+. Would Recommend.

THE CHAPESS

ISSUE #4

EXIS GROSS
RA JESELLA
RA SUTTERLIN
ISY LAFARGE
HEE WALL
KINNAMON
ELLA LUENG
RAH TODD
ACE DENTON
SE RIGGINS
UREN CROW
ARLOTTE MELLOR MEECHAM
CE SLATER
TH MAIDEN
NELIESE MACKINTOSH
ARLY MORRIS
NNAH BUCKMAN

Q+A with Cherry Styles

How did you get involved with self publishing?

I have always made stuff, and been involved with lots of creative projects (both for fun and as paid work.) I grew up in the South East of England and as a teenager definitely felt part of the DIY scene. I was lucky enough to have a supportive weirdo community around me, but I was well into my 20s before I really had more than a handful of female friends, or reason to question that. Working on the Chapess zine, particularly, gave me a way in, an excuse to get in touch with women I admired but was otherwise totally intimated by. I met Steve and Liz who run Salford zine library after I moved to Manchester a few years ago and along with Ingrid of Mythologising Me zine we've become a super tight team. This summer we're putting on the second Northwest Zine Fest as well as a bunch of exhibitions, workshops and readings too. We're all genuinely enthusiastic in a pretty old school way, we're passionate about spreading the word of self publishing and encouraging others to get involved. It's not an elitist group. There are no particular skills or experience required, anyone with a pen and an idea can make a zine.

In high school I made lots of covers for zines, and was always coming up with names for zines. The first one that actually had any pages was called Cheesey Smash + Salad Cream. I was 15, maybe 16 and I'd decided if I put together a music fanzine, like reviews of bands and albums I liked I could maybe get to meet some boys in bands under the vague suggestion that I was 'interviewing' them for my zine. It worked! I made some friends, learnt a few things the hard way.

So is zine making your job, or...?

No. I graduated from the now defunct Visual Studies course at Norwich Art School in 2008 and since then I've worked in education in one way or another, with varying levels of both responsibility and enthusiasm. In the last year or so I've been able to work on more ambitious publishing projects after kind of re-jigging my work life and going totally freelance.

Why self publish?

I think the thing with zines which really sets them apart in a positive way to more mainstream publications is that it's all kind of trial and error. There are no stakes. If you make something and decide you hate it, or it doesn't materialise in the way you imagined, just move onto the next thing, learn from your experiences. In making a zine you are effectively your own boss, editor, distributor etc. Self publishing is POLITICAL and POWERFUL!

Are there any difficulties or frustrations with zine making?

I think there are reasons people choose to self publish that will always remain the same, a need for greater control over the media we consume/produce, for financial/practical reasons, and for fun. There's definitely a new breed of zine makers, in the UK at least; many of them ambitious graduates who see zine making as a way to propel themselves into the mainstream press. Brands have begun co-opting the word zine to their own ends, there's a lot of misappropriation of the word going on. But I guess that's just how culture evolves.

I try to lead by example, put out the stuff i want to see, amplify the voices that matter to me, without patronising. It's not for everyone, it's a zine, and that's kind of the bottom line, i don't have anything riding on selling copies or anything like that, i'm not pandering to popular opinion to shift a product. Making zines is just one of things i do.

What's this surge in feminist zine making collectives all about?

Women and queers have always done this stuff. I think it's easier now with the internet for people to connect, younger people especially. Logistically it can make it easier to spread the word about your project, to pool resources and support one another in practical ways.

The recent attention zines have been getting in the mainstream press is interesting, and of course not without its own set of frustrations. I mean of course it's cool that more people get to see the stuff we're making. The term DIY culture as well as 'zine' itself is becoming almost a meaningless buzz word in a lot of contexts. But i'm a grown woman, I recognise bullshit when i see it.

I think it's important for us to have a platform that is not permeated by (straight,white) men in the way much of everyday live is. And i think within these working groups (eg. presses/readers) we are contributing to a more a positive model of female friendship and trust. I have kind of conflicting ideas about it, because of course i want my work to exist within different contexts and being a woman is just one of the ways i identify, but working in this kind of way has helped me to get to that point for sure.

Why DIY?

DIY comes out of necessity; this is just the way I've always done things. I would say that's true of a lot of us. Perhaps the reason the community is so welcoming is because we're all so relieved to have found each other. It's definitely validating to see other people working on similar projects. I would still make zines if I didn't have the community, but I probably would never know if anyone read them, or liked them, and would maybe spend too much time worrying about those things.

What's been the greatest benefit to getting involved with zines as both a creator and a reader?

Zines literally changed my life. Working on the Chapess, particularly has had a huge impact on my creative output. I've met so many ace people and had opportunities do all sorts of things as a direct result of it. I would recommend zine making to anyone who wants to get more involved with their community, get more politically engaged or just meet some new people. I have learnt, and am still leaning so much from zines.

I took over as sole editor of the Chapess in 2013 after Zara (Chapess zine founder) had her daughter Florence. The evolution of the zine has directly reflected the stuff I'm into and given me a platform to kind of do that publicly and share the stuff I love with an audience. In the last year or so it's really become a lit project, as reading and writing eclipsed visual art/photography in my life.

So how did the Chapess come about?

The zine was started by my friend and colleague Zara Gardner in the summer of 2011. We had both been involved with zines, art + the local DIY scene and wanted to bring our enthusiasm for self publishing into the classroom - so we decided to make a collective zine with our students and some of the other staff (at a sixth form college.) We both felt strongly that we wanted to help make feminism relevant to younger girls, especially those in rural areas/with limited resources as we had been. As a teen zines provided me with content i wasn't finding elsewhere, and I still think they have the capacity to do that.

I think it's important to arm young people with the tools they need to navigate the world for themselves - to make feminism relevant to young people, like it's not some inaccessible academic idea it's something that can directly change the way you view yourself and your circumstances and give you a framework to change them.

There aren't really any guidelines for submissions in terms of content for the Chapess, how do you choose what to include?

I feel like with each issue I put together the stuff gets better, but maybe folks just know the kind of stuff to send me. In the early days i imagined people submitting after reading the zine, maybe kind of in response to the pieces. Or it would give them the push they needed to submit all that stuff they'd been scribbling in their journal that was maybe kind of like the piece they'd just read in the Chapess. I never really set out to try and collect a certain type of writing. Poetry especially was never something I thought I would be involved with; it always seemed really inaccessible to me. Being part of this kind of creative community has given me the chance, and the confidence to try out new stuff with my own work too.

What made you want to start distribute zines as well as make your own?

Ever rising postage costs mean a lot of the time it just doesn't make sense to buy zines from the US. I was in a position where I was able to swap to bunch of copies of my zines with friends overseas + I decided to run with it. I moved the distro from a shoe box to an online shop just over a year ago. Rather than just duplicate the stock of some of the other UK distros i wanted to offer a small rotating selection of stuff alongside my own zines. The stuff I stock is basically the zines I have enjoyed reading + want to share.

What would you say to someone thinking about making their first zine?

Go for it! However small or relatively non-existent your budget, your immediate community or contacts - none of these things are necessarily barriers when it comes to zine making. If you're unsure about the content/layout/whatever do a bit of research, find out what zines are/not interesting to you - maybe there's a zine library or zine fair happening near you, talk to people who make zines, most of us don't mind getting the odd email. Think about your intent + motivation for making a zine, you're not going to make any money from it but you have everything (else) to gain.

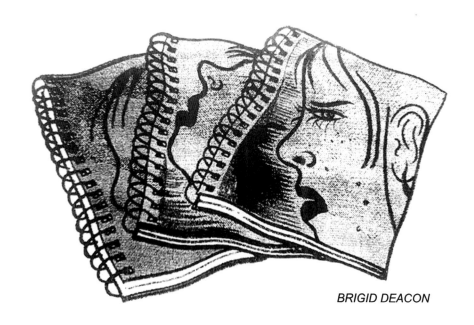

BRIGID DEACON

Originally I was going to sort of edit parts of this group interview, expand on reoccurring themes, or whatever. I wasn't really prepared for all the feelings you would all generously share. Maybe it seems like i'm kind of inflating my ego alone by doing this, but in the spirit of total transparency I decided to include it in full.

write anything you like about the Chapess (how did you become aware of it? what are your fav issues/pieces? have you found artists, writers, friends through the project?)

GD: The Chapess has been a regular light at the end of the tunnel for me. In the years when Cherry and I were separated by greater distance, it was a life line to her and the people she was excited by. It arrived on my doorstep and brought me back from the brink of full-time-job anxiety, it took off my blinkers that were telling me life and creativity are about gaining approval from men. It said "Fuck that!" in so many new ways. It got me through a manipulative relationship, a debilitating life-work-art balance, and then a starkly contrasted period of solitude too.

It can sometimes feel like "best friends" is a funny phrase to use in the later half of your twenties, but more and more I find myself using it to describe Cherry Styles. I am her's and she is mine. We are a perpetual gruesome twosome, in the background and the foreground of our minds. I am her soul sister and we feed our creativity in so many indefinable ways.

BD: hmm..okay yeah i think became aware of the chapess at a kind of pivotal moment, it felt really significant getting involved ~ i had just come out of a relationship and decided from then on to basically focus all the energy i had into relationships with women & nb, being the most amazing ppl in my life imaginable and most treasured relationships that they are, sources of the most life/mutual support/energy and joy, and everything else... it was like a big realisation and an affirmation. so at the same time, was making the first steps towards doing that and meeting new ppl & was hanging out w someone i met and they mentioned the chapess, but i'm not even sure that either of us had read it at that point, just heard loads of good stuff abt it? so i looked into it and saw that you posted about the grub zine and bc there were only a couple of copies left suddenly there was like an urgency to it...! so i messaged you asking if you still had any and you did and then sent it a note with it abt contributing to the chapess, and that was amazing , like I just was amazed and floored w how things could be that good, that quickly..! think there was something you put up a while ago that someone had said about yr generosity of spirit Cherry and i have to just second that bc that totally nails it, so much love straight in. can't describe the significance of what it has meant over the last few months, feel so full of love to get chatting and then be involved w this incredible thing you've brought together and so much into, and everything around it.. it's the most amazing thing. and all the stuff and bits we've been working on together since then... total dream tbh <3 <3

IB: I met Cherry and discovered The Chapess at Sheffield Zinefest! I think that it has a whole load of different things in that I like and haven't seen before but it's also a chance for people I am aware of in the zine community to write and have a voice in a way that is perhaps separate from what they do in their own work but also connected. Just a different sort of one off quality I feel, as some of the pieces are created especially for the zine.

SG: I followed the chapess blog on tumblr and was so excited and honoured when I was asked to be a part of an issue, I've always loved the DIY vibe and supporting women artists from all other the globe. My favourite issue is #6 because of the exhibition at doomed I was able to see a whole range of photography from bad ass ladies and it was very inspiring!

AG: I enjoy the concept of a strong platform for women to express themselves.

KU: I just think, knowing Cherry for as long as i have, that the chapess is on this evolutionary tip. It expresses a voice and a place that more and more girls/women/men want to hear, want to be a part of, and (importantly) *hope* exits out there in the world for them. I have discovered voices and messages that i don't always get to hear in my immediate surroundings and regardless of whether they are established or new, i value that. Every issue is exciting to physically hold in your hands -knowing there is something in there that will call out to you in that special way that honest things do.

AR: like many people, i 1st became aware of the Chapess through a kind of tumblr-osmosis. it began as a trickling stream, then a tidal wave. and now i can't imagine a time when you didn't exist. i don't think i can pick a favourite issue/piece but the 1st issue i actually bought was about 'work'. i loved that it had these little norwich references alongside fucking eileen myles, and everything in between. and i think there's a quote in it by Cheryl Strayed that i literally show to everyone. so yeah it's probably my most 'returned to' issue. i also feel attached to issue 5 because you published a piece of my writing, which i am of course so embarrassed about now, reading it back (but it's ok because this one marked the beginning of my mum's zine collection haha)

178

JK: My friend who lives in Amsterdam (Sofie) sent me a care package of lovely things, including a piece of her own original and gorgeouse art. she also sent me a copy of CHAPESS zine and i fell in love with it. I sat in the back yard on a sunday afternoon with our house cat sitting watch by my feet. I read it cover to cover and simply loved how many new bands i learnt about and the varied music history of females in punk history. I felt like the pages of CHAPESS zine was a world of amazing women who i could consider friends, confidants and partners in crime and creativity.

LS: I discovered the Chapess through Instagram and immediately identified with its female fervor. Since my initial Chapess discovery, I've been mind-fucked by Brigid Deacon's delightfully grimy artwork and countless other contributors who were willing to bare their teeth and let their socially-regulated smiles slip for a bit. Although I have not yet had the privilege of writing for the Chapess, my ode to Patti Smith was featured in the "Pissing in a River" fanzine, which was also curated by Ms Cherry Styles.

SS: The Chapess has influenced and inspired so much of myself, of my work. The range of content, of views, the sheer honesty makes it an important tribute to women everywhere.

SAZ: Someone on my tumblr reblogged that photo you have of a girl with the text "men will tell you things you love do not belong to you" and I was like wuuuuut waddup yassss. So i clicked the source to read more things and the things were so ridiculously in-your-face that i wanted to be part of it. My fave piece will always be that quote i mentioned above. I like how the chapess is unapologetically radical + feminist in a society where feminism is still a dirty word.

KF: I found the Chapess on tumblr and immediately loved the vibe - badass femmes making badass shit. I like that it's a zine, that it's physical, something you can hold in your hand. It's real.

KB: I got to know the Chapess through the illustrious Cherry. She got in touch with me through Tumblr and asked me if I would consider submitting some of my work for it. I submitted an altered version of my first ever published essay on Autostraddle 'It's Time For White Feminists To Stop Talking About Solidarity and Start Acting' and was thrilled to see it in print. My favourite issue is definitely #6 because not only is it the first issue I ever read, it has the best cover art! I bloody love that photo by Kelly Surdo and wish I had it blown up as a poster on my wall. Through the Chapess I've made a friend in Cherry who I barely deserve, she's just so fucking amazing?? She supports me unwaveringly, both personally and professionally and is always looking out for ways to help me out which is just a lovely feeling. I've never known anyone like her and I'm so glad that I have the privilege of calling her my friend to be honest. I'm always in awe of the cool shit she's doing and I admire her resolve infinitely.

AM: the chapess defines cool. i've found a friend in its creator, but i've also discovered writers and photographers that i now follow and pass along to others. the ultimate collection of creators to be a part of.

FD: I think Brigid Deacon is phenomenal.

CH: I found out about the project through one of my favourite resources, tumblr. I wanna keep contributing to every single issue as long as Cherry lets me. I work under the name SBTL CLNG, subtle ceiling. I'm a visual artist, illustrator, and writer. The 'writer' part is recent, though it's been an important part of my life + work for a long time. I'd never wanna call myself a writer because I never felt worthy or entitled to take up that kind of space. But recent projects and artists that've come into my life, like the Chapess, have validated and affirmed that I owe it to myself to take up that space in the world, especially as a non-White-male person. I self-publish zines and archive up tons of notes and little essays, collecting them for when they're ready. I draw everyday.

KI: On tumblr, I came across issue#4 with a portrait by Alexis Gross on the cover. It's such a great image. I began following thechapess on tumblr after that and shortly after I began submitting my own work.

IR: I found the Chapess through following Sara Sutterlin on Tumblr and immediately became interested and submitted straight away! I've been lucky enough to have my work featured twice. As an artist working very much within the institutional structures of the university/gallery it's so vital to experience an alternative to these spaces, online and offline. I find it a great source of inspiration to see how different people approach many of the same subjects that I make my work about in this format. I follow a lot of the contributors on social media outlets, Cherry is the only person who I've met irl but I felt really welcomed into the community and compelled to submit again!

SK: I first came across Chapess two years ago thanks to the weird & wonderful world of twitter & then met Cherry for the first time at North West Zine festival & I felt like I had known her for years, it was a lovely feeling.

SLD: I saw it floating around for awhile, but didn't get a copy until a couple of years ago when Cherry traded for some of my zines. My favourite issue is the current one, mostly because every dear friend of mine wrote an excellent piece and I love being reminded how great my friends are and how lucky I am t have them!

HJ: I came about The Chapess throughly Tumblr and was delighted when Cherry included a photo of my little sister wearing something I made as at the time I felt it was really significant to challenge beauty ideals and I'm so glad Cherry put it in The Chapess exhibition at Doomed Gallery. I think the whole zine is a wonderful collective of women and is truly inspiration and empowering.

E-BL: I stumbled upon the Chapess at Sheffield zine fair, drawn in by a Kathy Acker pic (I think on the front page if I remember). I instigated a zine trade after that and submitted some of my own pieces. I loved the theme some were tackling of how to fit creativity around work obligations (as that's been relevant to me lately).

LM: I first became aware of The Chapess when I used Tumblr (A LOT) when I was younger. I think Girls Get Busy zine reblogged something from you and I then went on to buy lots of the zines, and then saw you again at DIY Cultures at Rich Mix. I love the high quality of writing in The Chapess (esp. the personal/creative nonfiction essays) and the DIY aesthetics.

EH: I love that the Chapess exists. It makes me proud to be a woman writer and inspires me to self-publish more.

TS: What I most like about the Chapess is its poetics of inclusion. The Chapess is not a clique - you don't have to perform in any special way to be accepted. People are simply invited to share their creative expressions from the heart.

how would you describe the zine to a friend?

GD: The Chapess is a space where non-dudes can express something. Overseen by Cherry's careful eye, the zine gathers pace and prowess at an incredible rate. She pushes it forwards and into the hands of the right people, gaining notoriety with the respected people she manages to get within the pages, whilst still publishing exciting work from new voices that she has encouraged.

BD: this is such a hard one and that's ridiculous having described to friends many times and now i don't know how to sum it up haha. uh..whole-hearted, intense and real - unpretentious. idk.. fucking powerful..(the last two issues just hit so hard, like, riight in the guts ~ had to kind of sit back and cry it out and feel it all and then put it down -feeling stronger for it). Em ledger's piece and your convo with grace in the last one, were so so great... love love love sbtl clng's work. everything, really. (+ also really appreciate that there is actually so much work packed in and that it's not pricey despite that. zines shouldn't be. super important, too)

IB: A zine that comes out more than once a year, champions female artists and raises their work up for others to admire and absorb.

SG: Raw and uncensored and supportive of women - not afraid to portray women in a more real light in comparison than the pristine image the media creates.

AG: Photos and articles you need to see and read, not want, but need to.

KU: Bold, touching, honest, provocative, hopeful.

AU: I love the creativity of the female contributors, and Cherry's vision. Feminist writing at its best

AR: what is so perfect about the Chapess is how genuinely accessible, unpretentious and welcoming it is. i find myself reading it and just nodding along to things and yelling 'yeah!'

JK: A female smorgesboard of smart, articulate, creative, passionate brainy babes. You will get lost in a vortex of amazing and varied worlds. A womans mind is a power house and this zine allows it full and free reign; learn it, live it and love it.

LS: The Chapess zine is fiercely feral, subversive, and feminine. It's a literary gun to the head of patriarchy and a triumphant nod to female-identifying nonconformists everywhere.

SAZ: Punk feminism. The lesbian satanist art that made my grandparents and parents disown me and I'm cool with that.

KF: A punch in the face from a fist with painted fingernails

KB: bad bitches doing their own thing

AM: a collection of radical punk women expressing themselves

CH: A loving/rage filled nest carved out by women for women to uphold women and give life/light to women. A crucial space/void for healing and not feeling so goddamn alone.

KI: The Chapess is a platform for women artists/writers/creators to say what they feel and showcase their talents. A place where women can relate to one another through art, a safe place in which to be honest and open. I see the Chapess as a publication that portrays the strength and rebelliousness of women rather than the neat and feminine depictions we grew up seeing on tv and in magazines. To me, the Chapess highlights the fact that everyone's a little weird, a little off, but it's totally okay.

IR: Inclusive feminist punk zine w/ tonnes of amazing art/writing/music stuff.

SK: It's like a small journal that is being passed around, from a friend to another, filling it each time by their feelings, photographs, doodles until the journal is fully completed to the last page.

SLD: A collection of stuff that will make you wanna go out and make STUFF!

HJ: The Chapess is the sort of zine that you flick through and think, I'm gunna love this. Then when you get home and make a cuppa, sit down with ya cat and have a proper good read, you're like 'Finally a group of gals that get me!' Like I said in the previous question, truly empowering with a real sense of community and honest. I'm not too good with words but I'd tell my friends that it's my fave zine and then give it to them to borrow! :)

E-BL: Bold. Feminist. Wise. Women taking up space in the world. Real juicy and full of inspirational tangents to go chase up - musical and literary.

LM: I would describe it as carefully curated, interesting, pretty and a really good and informative read.

EH: It's a compilation zine of work by underground writers/artists/photographers who identify as female.

TS: It will surprise you with its ability to touch you on a deep level. The work is tender and tough.

write anything you like about community, do you feel part of a community online and/or IRL + how/does the Chapess factor into that?

GD: I feel like twitter and instagram and tumblr contribute to my ever-growing feeling that the world is full of girls who are intelligent, fierce, creative and electric. As if I had ever doubted that! But it's easy to feel alone when you're surrounded by men, and put into competition with the women in your scene. Feel like online ~bonding (or just reading and appreciating) has really strengthened a lot of non-male people's resolve, and formed a sprawling, shifting community that's always welcoming yet self-critical too. Feel like the way Cherry has used the chapess and synchronise witches pages on all these platforms has put me in touch with a lot of great people, and made me aware of so many new ways of thinking and feeling about the world.

BD: Yeah deffo feel a sense of community around the chapess, i think just since getting involved and even by following probably everyone's work that i've come across through the chapess and everything surrounding it!. really feel like seeing, reading, people's art, writing, work, conversations about and around things like mental health/trauma/feminism(s)/sexuality have meant so much bc for some reason i always felt like those aspects of work/presented self had to be sidelined/ kept to a minimum and getting involved in the chapess and stuff around it has felt kind of huge and beautiful and liberating in that respect, too. it's been a really huge thing. hard to describe how much that means. :)

IB: I don't really use tumblr cos it's ~overwhelming~ and I think that it is a key community when it comes to the chapess. I am not sure if I am the average chapess reader but actually this intrigues me as to what the average chapess reader is actually like. A feminist with flaws and the recognition of their own flaws, down with intersectionality, unapologetic about their presence but also sensitive and a good listener. Would like to meet. Idk because the chapess is essentially a compzine and in essence a directory of women and girls I might like to meet. There is sometimes this feeling of people writing zines being cool without knowing that yes, their email is at the back of the zine and yes maybe you should email the contributor whose work you like the most and say it affected you or made you feel less alone. Maybe that's something I will do now.

AG: With bad there is good and vice versa. The Internet gives people an opportunity to hop on shit blindly that they have no genuine connection to. When I come across something such as the Chapess that separates the real from the fake, I can truly appreciate that. LA lacks community like NY but in the end you are your own best friend. I like that and tend to keep myself away from online and IRL cliques. I just do my thing and don't worry about what anyone else is doing.

KU: Well. I've always had a little trouble being part of certain communities and still feel that that is a consistent, albeit less frustrating, aspect of my life. Chapess is like a solace, a safe place where i can and i can see other humans indulging (not in the self obsessed way) aspects of themselves that they might otherwise be made to feel ashamed of, that they shouldn't actually be. Especially IRL. The fact that that place exists, if you really think about it, is a physical interruption and a real alternative to what those dominant narratives tell us. Our voices don't matter and to express them makes no difference to their power in shaping the world. Fuck that shit.

AR: after graduating art school a few years ago i didn't really find a place in the 'art world' or the 'publishing world'. the Chapess is definitely responsible for helping me feel like part of the 'zine community'. like all it takes is going to a fair or buying something from an online distro. continual sharing, never entertaining sleekness or exclusivity. i mean i think you are kind of like everyone's cool older sister you know?

JK: I do feel part of a few amazing communities here in Melbourne. I feeel part of the feminist community and the disability feminist community (intersectionality IS SO IMPORTANT) i feel a part of a live music community (sort of, as a fan of female fronted bands and endeavore to support them in any way i can, even if they play on a tuesday night x) Im lucky to live in melbourne as there are some great female fronted bands such as Maureen

The pink tiles Ouch my face Courtney Barnett The girl fridas Ghost dick Primm CHAPESS is something i admire greatly and i am warmed and comforted by the community it engages in. I would love to get more involved in the community it creates. I would love to contribute to that community. thank you CHAPESS and i hope to contribute soon.

LS: The online community that women and girls have cultivated for themselves through art and writing is fucking grand. I think that there's a certain kind of power in the celebration of feminine vulnerability and exposure that's unique to the female experience. This online community has ultimately given voice to the silenced. I've been able to share thoughts through a few platforms, mainly Zine Club Mag (http://www.zineclubmag.com), which is edited by Rookie Mag contributor Alyson Williams. Zine Club Mag is one of the many female-fronted platforms that make up a virtual communal bath of vulnerability and affirmation. I especially identify with the Chapess because it's an extension of deviance with regards to the likes of Kathy Acker, Patti Smith, and Kathleen Hanna. It's punk, powerful, and anything but polite.

SS: So much of what we consume as women does not reflect our identities at all. Mostly we're bombarded with ideas on how to be Better versions of ourselves. The Chapess and the feminist online community most of us are part of provide vital reflections of women and women's work.

SAZ: I must say Im not very good at making friends or being part of a social circle as I get all anxious and paranoid. But Cherry has always been very chill and nice and I am grateful for that.

KF: I love watching the community grow - I found out about the zine online, I got some poems in, told my friends about it, they submitted, they got some poems in - I like watching the circles of influence expand.

KB: I used to live in Brighton and definitely became wary of the idea of feminist/queer communities because I saw how that resolutely wasn't the case in the city. There was so much animosity and fractions/factions. So when I moved up North I was so pleasantly surprised to see that the queers up here practice what they preach and it's through women like Cherry and Beth Maiden (issue #4 contributor and all round great gal) that I've been able to see what it's like to have women around who are truly supportive and kind-hearted.

AM: i would actually suffocate and die in the suburbs if it wasn't for punk communities and outlets, online and off. the chapess gives me air to breathe easy when i'm the only girl in town with the guts to wear black combat boots.

FD: I think community develops best when there's shared endeavor. A creative community creates community!

IR: I found that there were connections between Chapess and other publications I like such as SALT and I like how content circulates around these networks, feels like there is a v. good community of likeminded creative women/people sharing and supporting each other. I don't have a big network of people online who I interact with, but i'm happy to be on the periphery and lucky to be introduced to many of these artists through the Chapess.

SK: I feel like meeting Cherry & reading the Chapess has made me embrace a lot of things that I wouldn't have otherwise, especially moving into a different environment & culture where everything is so open, & I still sometimes ask myself "am I doing this right?", but being in this zine community has also provided me with a lot of confidence.

SLD: Looking back I realise I have made so many of my best friends through the zine community some how. And that I continue to do, even with the shift from connection via letters to connection via the internet. I feel that the Chapess however has brought me a small creative community in the city I live in.

HJ: that's totally how I would describe The Chapess, a community in print format! A collective of women that work together rather than compete with one another. I definitely feel part of a strong girl power community when I read The Chapess and I feel like there should be zines like this in schools and stuff, as I feel the content is very educational to helping develop your own self esteem and encouraging creative self expression. Big shout out to Cherry, you are a star! :)

LM: I feel part of an online community of amazing women who are doing incredible things in zines and writing and am organising the feminist riot grrrl #genesisters night which hosts feminist bands and zine stalls (including The Chapess for the May event!) and DJs which I'm hoping will bring that sort of culture together IRL!

EH: The only community I feel like I belong to is the zine community which exists online, through our zines and through letters sent. I honestly can't imagine my life without this community: it's a safety net for when times are tough; we inspire each other to create; help each other live our lives. The Chapess is part of this community. It's proof that it exists (as if any were needed!)

CH: Community is this idea I'm always really homesick for, always longing for. But I realize now that community and the support they give doesn't just happen out of thin air, it actually takes a lot of intention- maintaining connections, exchanging knowledge, checking in on folks, being transparent. The internet has helped so much with this and has actually given me so much support that I don't always feel irl. I met some really potent friends through sharing/blogging online. Ken Cee (varsityqueerleadercaptain.tumblr.com) found my art online and started reblogging it and I was like: Oo who is this? We started an irl to url friendship off of tumblr and now they're a very real factor in my "irl" life. Same with Lora Mathis- they just contacted me about contributing to a zine and we happened to both be in L.A. the same night and just went for it, met, and totally bonded-

and it all happened because we both publish our output online. Online I'm able to stay in touch and see what my friends are up to up in the Bay Area, what's going on with my friends making things on the East coast, in Texas, in England (hey Cherry /VV), etc. It's all really potent, this global crossover of the virtual terrain into the physical terrain. So maybe at the end of the day I do have more community than I think I do. The Chapess is a definitely a factor in this- I always look forward to contributing to every new issue and feel like my work has a home in that zine, among all those talented and potent artists. It's a fucked up time in the world but damn, it's also a really exciting time to be alive and making art.

the chapess

Issue #1 cover: Zara Gardner

the chapess

Issue 2

cover: Zara Gardner

the chapess

the WORK issue

Karis Upton
Riese Bernard
Cáit Fahey
Jen Steiner
Grace Hong
Jo Stafford
Molly Davy
Eileen Myles
Cherry Styles
Sophie Cooper
Zara Gardner
Abbi Cudden
Donna Shapiro

cover: Cherry Styles

THE CHAPESS

ISSUE #5

cover: Lauren Cook

THE CHAPESS

ISSUE #6

cover: Kelly Surdo

192

THE CHAPESS
ISSUE #7

cover: Jane Cardiet

THE CHAPESS
ISSUE #8

cover: Emma Kohlmann

THE CHAPESS
ISSUE #9

cover: Brigid Deacon

GUT FLORA

A CHAPESS ZINE COLLECTION

SYNCHRONISE
WITCHES PRESS

SALFORD ZINE LIBRARY PRESENTS

THE CHAPESS ZINE #8 LAUNCH

MINI ZINE FEST

LADYFEST DJs

AS PART OF MANCHESTER POPFEST
SATURDAY 15TH AUGUST FROM 2·30
KRAAK SPACE, STEVENSON SQUARE M1 1DB

poster artwork by Brie Moreno   194

The Chapess zine 2011-2016

Hira Mahmood, Lucia Canuto, Andrea Quinlan, Jolie M-A, Jessica Mendham, Jocine Velasco, Naomi Baguley, Lydia B, Georgia Grace Gibson, Lauren Cook, Bruna Massadas, Sofija M. Gugina, Ele-Beth Little, Suzy X, Alejandra Pombo, Ella Dawson, Iris Sidikman, Inma Lorente, Sofia Yuriko Baca , Bea Macdonald, Sara Sutterlin, Alicia Rodriguez , Gabrielle Giuliano, Britt Hatzius, Claire Grossman, Sade Andria Zabala, Allison McKelvey, Jessie Askinazi, Adrienne Arcilla, Jessie Lynn McMains, Cheyenne Sophia, Ellie Power, Maegan Hill-Carroll , Eva Silverman , Briana de la Torre, Elizabeth Scrase , Barbara Moses, Sarah Hopp, Kelly Surdo, Jane Chardiet, Chloe Sugden, Molly Matalon, Alba Yruela, Dana Goldstein, Katie Foster, Sahar Gilani, Kayla Day, Ingrid Boring, Melanie King, Alyssa Rorke, Julia Scheele, Jessie Lynn McMains, Alexis Gross, Miyako Bellizzi, Joy Martin, Kesiena Boom, Sara Sutterlin, Allison Maloney, Sarah Edwards, Iona Roisn, Charlotte McHarg, Georgie Watts, Sarah Zapata, SBTL CLNG, Elizabeth Scott, Szilvia Molnar, Catch Business, Sharon Green, Chloe Burns, Heather Dunlop, Karen Isaac, Sarah Christie, Leslie Boroczk, Eleanor Bleier, Inney Mallard, Kendra Sullivan, Morgan Maher, Emma Thacker, the Shruggals, Isabella Bestfriend, Kelsey Henderson, Louise Woodcock, Aimee Wall, Kara Jesella, Daisy LaFarge, Liz Kinnamon, Stella Lueng, Sarah Todd, Grace Denton, Jesse Riggins, Lauren Crow, Charlotte Mellor Meecham, Alice Slater, Beth Maiden, Anneliese Mackintosh, Charly Morris, Hannah Buckman, Emma Kohlmann, Lou McQuillan, SJ Bradley, Julia Wohlstetter, Tracy Struck, Saffa Khan, Angharad Williams, Alanna McArdle, Emma Woll-Wenzel, Claire Askew, Ember Small, Morgan Sturgeon, Elizabeth Hall, Stacey-Marie Piotrowski, Frances Cannon, Lily Myers, Julia Feige, Martha PW, Em Ledger, Brigid Deacon, Marlo Koch, Eva Marie Nelson, Hannah Regel, Joana Matias, Karen Isaac, Maddie Goldbeck, Emily Bueckert, Victoria Manifold, Alison Rhea,Emma Hacking, Ayshe Uzunoglu, Jessica Knight, Lydia Sviatoslavsky, Francis Dawson, Seleena Laverne Daye, Laura Maw, Devin Utah, Madge Maril, Tammy Mercure, Kate

195

Armitage, Hannah Mort, Rachel
Woroner, Liisa Morton, Valeria
Picerno, Ruth Ossai, Sadie Rees
Hales, Isabella Martin, Harriet
Broom, Roshni Bhagotra, Shannei
Brown, Ines Berra Viola, Elisabeth
Perez, Rhiannon Parkinson, Emily
Tulett, Miranda La Mere, Briana
Frazer, Jessie Dinan, Milana
Zadworny, Helena Juric, Maddi
Montero, Veronika Pot, Ruth
McMillan, Megan Eagles, Eva
Paia, Marisa Gertz, Victoria
Lincoln, Karis Upton, Riese
Bernard, Cait Fahey, Jen Steiner,
Grace Hong, Jo Stafford, Molly
Davy, Eileen Myles, Sophie
Cooper, Zara Gardner, Abbi
Cudden, Ruby Ratafia, Misty Pane,
Anna Anon, Betsy Hatter, Beth
Morrison, Lucy Abel, Hels Bells,
A.Stone, Deb O'Nair, Loretta De La
Coeur, Lizzy Campbell, Helen
Entwhistle, Natalie Bradbury, Kay
Richards, Helen Piercy, Gemma
Correll, Becky Garratt, Christa
Harris, Miriam Nice, Vicki Johnson,
Nicola Renshaw

A huge thank you to everyone who
has supported the zine over the
last 5 years + to everyone who
pre-orederd a copy of this book,
which has made the first printing
possible.

Special thanks to For Books' Sake
for their support + encouragement
putting this book together, Matt and
Ken at Doomed gallery, Steve, Liz
+ Ingrid at Salford Zine Library.
Especially big thanks to JB.

printed by the lovely folks
at Ex Why Zed
www.exwhyzed.co.uk